FOLKLORE
from the
ADIRONDACK FOOTHILLS

PROSPECT BOOKS
By HOWARD THOMAS

THE LIFE OF A VILLAGE (1950)
TRENTON FALLS, YESTERDAY & TODAY (1951)
MARINUS WILLETT: SOLDIER-PATRIOT (1954)
TALES FROM THE ADIRONDACK FOOTHILLS (1956)
FOLKLORE FROM THE ADIRONDACK FOOTHILLS (1958)
BOYS IN BLUE FROM THE ADIRONDACK FOOTHILLS (1960)
BLACK RIVER IN THE NORTH COUNTRY (1963)
THE SINGING HILLS (1964)
THE ROAD TO SIXTY (1966)
JOSEPH BRANT (THAYENDANEGEA) (1973)

FOLKLORE from the ADIRONDACK FOOTHILLS

by Howard Thomas
sketches by John D. Mahaffy

PROSPECT
BOOKS
1980

© Howard Thomas 1958

The Melancholy Walker, copyright, 1946, by Liberty Magazine.

No Night for Singing, copyright, 1947, by Liberty Magazine.

ISBN 978-0-913710-02-9

FOREWORD

A book should have a reason for publication. The purpose of this series of folklore tales is to bring to the attention of the present generation a way of life which has almost departed from the Adirondack foothills. Logs no longer hurtle down the amber rivers in the spring, the horse-drawn vehicle seldom is seen on the roads, and the wheels of the gristmills and sawmills have long been inactive. Cracker-barrel sages have departed from the country stores, and those peculiar breeds of men, the tramps and the hermits, have disappeared from the highways and the forests.

In *Tales from the Adirondack Foothills,* published two years ago, I tried to give an overall picture of the chronology of the foothills through the use of short tales. *Folklore from the Adirondack Foothills* attempts to portray phases of life in the area which extends from the Mohawk River to the Adirondack Mountains. Purists may argue that all of the yarns are not folklore, but most of the tales have found their roots in the lives of the people.

The use of poetry and fiction in a book of folklore is also open to criticism which I shall make no attempt to defend. The sonnets which introduce each section were written to satisfy a lifelong desire to write in that form. I admit that the result will not make William Wordsworth turn over in his grave. The four stories which comprise the last section of the book are fiction, but fiction based upon what I heard and saw while spending boyhood summers in Prospect. My grandfather actually ran a stone quarry. Italian laborers built the railroad, and I heard a glorious voice from atop grandfather's corncrib. Goshen Hall stood across the road from grandfather's house and was the scene of many a village entertainment. The characters in the stories are fictitious, and if they bear any resemblance to persons living or dead, it is purely coincidental.

In gathering material for this book, I am indebted to the *Boonville Herald,* which gave me access to its file of newspapers, and to the librarians in Utica and Rome, who gladly put at my disposal material from which certain tales evolved. I am also grateful to numerous individuals

FOREWORD

who supplied folklore and who are mentioned in connection with the tales.

Grateful acknowledgment is made to Lorraine Lester, New York, for permission to reprint my stories, *The Melancholy Walker* and *No Night for Singing,* which were published in *Liberty Magazine* September 7, 1946 and August 2, 1947, respectively, of which she is the copyright owner.

HOWARD THOMAS

CONTENTS

		Page
	Foreword	v
I	ROADS	1
	COACH AND FOUR	3
	HI JINKS IN NORWAY	5
	THE CORPSE WANTED A DRINK	7
	BLACK HOLLOW	9
	ON TO PISECO!	11
	A COUPLE OF GINGERS	13
	BORROWED TRANSPORTATION	15
	SUMMER VISITORS	17
	THE TANTALIZING TRAMP	19
II	STREAMS	21
	"WHOO-EE-EE! THE PUSSY-WILLOW!"	23
	THE FABULOUS CARNAHANS	25
	RIDING WITH DEATH	29
	THE DOD BLIMPED STERK	32
	THRILLING RESCUES	33
	COURT GOT A CHASER	35
	THE GHOST OF THE KUYAHOORA	36
III	SAWMILLS	37
	SEA SERPENT?	39
	SABBATH IN HINCKLEY	41
	STALEMATE	43
	ROBINSON THE GREAT	45
	WILD BILL AND THE WOODCHOPPERS	47
	FIRE IN THE NIGHT	49
	LITTLE ITALY	51
	UNCLE TOM'S CABIN	53

IV	**FOLKS**	55
	THE SEARCH	57
	THE LONG-HAIRED ORATOR	59
	OLD MORRIS	61
	A PRESIDENT COMES HOME	63
	BOONVILLE GETS A FAIR	65
	"FURRINERS"	67
	THE UBIQUITOUS REDHEAD	69
	WHAT'S IN A NAME?	71
	THE VALUABLE COAT	73
	WELSH CONFUSION	75
	MORE ABOUT DINGLE DANGLE	77
	ALLIE	79
	THE BEDSIDE MANNER	81
	LAURIE BACH	83
V	**MURDER**	85
	A MAD CLERIC	87
	DARK NIGHT IN NORTH WESTERN	90
	LOCK 66	93
	CEDAR JOHN	97
VI	**NORTH WOODS**	99
	WHY GUGUGLE LAKE WENT DRY	101
	ROC HATED BEARS	103
	THE PESKY CROWS	107
	IKE'S BEAVER	109
	THE BEAR HOAX	111
	"PANTHUR"	113
	WALT'S TWO-WAY HOUND	116
VII	**FICTION**	117
	NO NIGHT FOR SINGING	119
	THE CHALLENGE SOLO	127
	WRONG SCENT	134
	THE MELANCHOLY WALKER	142

FOLKLORE
from the
ADIRONDACK FOOTHILLS

I. ROADS

The foothills roads wind over hill and dale,
Skirt woodland tracts and cross the rushing streams.
Upon them oft the brilliant sunlight gleams,
Or rain or snow or glist'ning winter hail.
The stage coach rocked along them with the mail,
To carry settlers to their land of dreams;
And tramps and wand'rers aired some paltry schemes
That caused the frugal housewives oft to wail.

To you who read about the days of yore
And recreate once more the distant scene,
I offer tales which have been told before,
Though some the light of print have never seen.
I hope to entertain and not to bore.
On you, dear reader, judgment has to lean.

COACH AND FOUR

The first roads into the Adirondack foothills consisted of mere tracks through the wilderness. Baron Steuben constructed one from Herkimer to his holdings at Sixty Acres, and Gerrit Boon carved a trail from Fort Schuyler (Utica) to Oldenbarneveld and later to Remsen and Boonville. French emigres cut across the Steuben Hills to High Falls (Lyons Falls) and Castorland.

The first highway to enter the foothills was the State Road, which rambled across hills and valleys from Johnstown to Sackets Harbor during the first decade of the nineteenth century. A few years later, the Black River Turnpike from Utica intersected the State Road at the Black River House, about four miles north of Remsen village, and followed the earlier road to Watertown.

Stages left Utica at ten in the morning and got through to Sackets Harbor in a day. The journey to Ogdensburg could be made in two days. The speediest stage trip from Utica to Sackets Harbor took place on February 19, 1829. Though the ground was covered with two and a half feet of snow, the stage covered the 93 miles in nine hours and forty-five minutes, including stops for changing mail at post offices.

The stages, with bodies supported upon strap-strings, rocked and swayed as the wheels bounced through the rutted roads. The passengers rode inside the coach, with their baggage held by a leather-covered rack in the back known as the "boot."

Stage drivers handled the reins from seats high up in the front of the coach and were amazingly skillful at manipulating reins on four and sometimes six horses. It is probably true that an expert driver could brush a fly off a lead horse's ear with a flick of the wrist, and that the cracking of his whip sounded like explosions of firecrackers.

M. F. Roberts writes in his *History of Remsen:* "The arrival of the stage was the great event of the day. The driver would sound his horn as he approached. With a loud crack of his long lashed whip over the heads of his horses to accelerate their speed into town, he would circle up to the door of the tavern with a grand flourish, throw the reins to a hostler in waiting, and descending from his high seat on the top of the coach, walk with the dignity of a general into the house. It was not until he had removed the dust and grime of the trip, and sauntered back to the bar-room, that any could have the boldness to ask for news."

Horses were changed about every fifteen miles, stops for this purpose being made at Skinner's in Trenton, Black Hawk Higby's five miles above Remsen, Dick Hulbert's in Boonville, and at Leyden Hill, Houseville and Lowville.

Medad Hoyt and John Hicks, the veterans of the route, were inclined to baby their horses; George Carver was particularly proud of his matched lead horses, dark chestnuts with white manes and tails; Ed Bush had a bay mare on his wheel team which would draw for no other driver. Each driver had a tin horn which he blew in a distinctive manner, so folks in the villages always knew which man was on the high seat long before the stage arrived.

Tavern keepers along the road became noted for jovial good-fellowship. Isaac Curry not only kept tavern in South Trenton but he also acted as toll collector on the turnpike. Elizur Skinner put up a hotel in Trenton which he and his family operated for over fifty years. In Prospect, Matt Hoyt and Asa McMaster catered to travellers on the State Road. Jake Lewis, the famous storyteller, held forth in Remsen. Five miles north of that village, Oliver (Black Hawk) Higby was famous for his oyster dinners.

The best-known of all the tavern keepers lived in Boonville. Richard Hulbert entertained celebrities passing through the foothills for over thirty years. General U. S. Grant stopped at Dick's place, as did General Phil Sheridan and Horace Greeley. Strange to say, Hulbert's Hotel, as it was called, had no bar, but was noted for its excellent rooms and meals.

Hulbert was more than a tavern keeper. He made the principal address at the opening of the Black River Railroad, presided when the Conkling Rifles left for the Civil War, was elected to the state assembly and served as county clerk. He owned a lumber business in Boonville and a mill on the Black River near Hawkinsville. All Boonville was saddened when the multiplicity of enterprises brought financial embarrassment to Dick and to the friends who had backed him. Of all the early tavern keepers, his name alone is retained in the present Hulbert House in Boonville.

HI JINKS IN NORWAY

Early settlers in Norway usually attended church on Sunday, but they gave vent to rural humor during the week. Uncle Nezer Sweet got quite enthusiastic about Universalism and liked to preach that doctrine. A neighbor invited him to supper, and Uncle Nezer was holding forth on his favorite subject. To emphasize a point he said, "I feel as certain of going to heaven as I do of eating this piece of meat." As he raised his knife, the piece of meat slipped off, fell to the floor and was gobbled up by a hungry dog.

Uncle Nezer's Universalism did not prevent him from working on the Sabbath, something that simply was not being done in Norway. The old fellow became ill, but was on the road to recovery when Jake Du-Bois returned from church to find Nezer working in his potato patch.

"Why, Mr. Sweet," said DuBois, "you promised if you got well you would stop working on Sunday."

Uncle Nezer leaned on his hoe handle and replied, "Yes, so I did, but then I ain't quite well yet."

Ump Ferris also liked to play hooky on Sunday, so one fine summer day he went fishing over on Spruce Creek. On his way home with a fine string of trout, he saw Elder Bowles striding down the road on his way home from church. Ump sat down on a stone wall and let his string of fish dangle behind it.

"Mr. Ferris," asked the elder, "can you pasture my horse a few weeks? I want to turn him out."

Ump put on his most solemn face and answered, "Elder Bowles, I don't care to talk about secular matters on the Sabbath."

The Ferris family settled early in Norway and produced some famous men, including the co-founder of Knox College in Galesburg, Illinois, and the inventor of the Ferris wheel which entertains children at carnivals. Some of them had a cantankerous streak, however. Two Ferris boys were tending the family sugarbush when Pack Whitford's dog came along. The boys hated this particular dog, so they killed it and put the carcass under a brush heap. Whitford found out about it but bided his time. The run of sap was good that year, and the boys were kept busy boiling it in the huge iron kettle. One night they got sleepy, so they left the kettle boiling and went home to bed. When they got back in the morning, something had been added to the syrup—the carcass of Pack Whitford's dog. They suspected Pack, but all they could get out of him was, "Well, that dog of mine always did like sweet."

Independence Day usually brought about a celebration in Norway. Harp Johnson, a hater of work and a lover of hunting and fishing, bought a supply of powder at Fred Mason's store. He came in the day before the holiday and complained, "Squire Mason, that powder I bought ain't good for nothing. It got wet and I spread it out before the fire to dry, and a coal snapped into it, and before I could go to the spring for water to put it out, more than half of it burned up." Harp did not miss the celebration. Axe in hand and with a flag wrapped around his middle, he climbed a tall hemlock, lopping off limbs as he went up, and floated the Stars and Stripes from the top of the tree.

The Cook brothers later kept the largest store in Norway. It served for town meetings, elections and village gatherings. One Fourth of July, celebrants collected material for a grand sendoff. Among the articles was a blacksmith's anvil that was to serve as a cannon. When the time came, no anvil was in sight. John Coe, who was watching preparations through narrowed eyes, heard, along with the others, the distant sound of the cannon going off in a marsh a mile from the village.

"Wonder what calf is bleating," commented Coe, who had dragged the anvil to the marsh and had hired a friend to touch it off at a given time.

Winter also brought a touch of whimsy to Norway. Jared Smith had spent an evening in Mason's store. On the way home, he got caught in a driving blizzard. As he battled his way through the storm, his hat flew off and whirled across the drifts beyond recovery.

When he came home hatless, his wife asked, "Jared, where is your hat?"

"Gone to the devil," growled Jared.

"Never mind, Jared," said his wife soothingly. "You will surely find it."

THE CORPSE WANTED A DRINK

Miss Soloma Whiting, a tall, graceful young woman, taught school in Norway in 1817. Soloma was popular with young and old, and after the local grapevine had spread the news that she was engaged to marry young Harvey Willoughby, the whole village registered pleasure. When Soloma took sick and died within a few days, most of the villagers attended her burial service in White Creek Cemetery.

A few days later, citizens were shocked to learn that ghouls had visited the cemetery and had removed Soloma's body. Fingers were pointed in the direction of nearby Fairfield College for Physicians and Surgeons, for students were known to remove bodies from graves for dissecting purposes.

Norway rose up as one man. Several meetings were held, and a semi-military company was formed to go to Fairfield and demand Soloma's body. Chosen as captain was Josh Paul, a stalwart, daring fellow who feared no one. The company assembled, armed with muskets, scythes and other weapons. Someone had brought a cannon. Paul cried, "On to Fairfield!" and the angry avengers followed him on the double-quick.

The authorities at Fairfield had gotten wind of the proposed invasion, so they prepared to defend the buildings. When Paul and his company drew up on the campus, the Fairfield doctors denied that any of their students had stolen Soloma's body. This obvious lie was greeted with hoots and catcalls. Paul drew up his men in battle array and pointed the cannon at one of the buildings. Blood might have been shed if the Fairfield authorities had not seen the handwriting on the wall— or maybe on the cannon. They asked for a conference with Paul. Peace was declared when they handed Soloma's body over to him.

The Norway army returned triumphantly with Soloma's body, which they reburied. They still did not trust Fairfield, so young men took turns guarding the grave nights until the danger of other grave-robbers appearing had passed.

The sport of grave-robbing also had its humorous aspects. A Prospect legend indicates that the village beside the waterfall was also involved in this practice. As the story goes, a stranger drove up to McMaster's tavern at the lower end of the village late at night. Two young fellows saw the horse and wagon pull into the shed. They felt sure that two men had been in the vehicle and that only one had gotten out to go into the tavern, so they went into the shed to investigate.

Sure enough, a blanketed figure was sitting rigidly on the wagon seat. They spoke to it, and when it did not answer, they prodded it and it slumped over on the seat. They unwrapped the blanket and discovered that it had covered the dead body of a man.

The young fellows could have rushed into the tavern and denounced the grave-robber, but they put their heads together and decided to teach the ghoul a lesson he would never forget. One of them took the blanket off the body, wrapped it around his own shoulders, and took his place on the wagon seat, while the other fellow lifted the body from the wagon and hid it in the shed.

The drinker came out of the tavern, took his seat beside the blanketed figure, and backed the horse out of the shed. The prankster who remained behind nodded his head significantly when he saw the horse and wagon start toward Boon's Bridge, which led across the West Canada Creek toward Russia and Fairfield.

The night was black as ink and the roar from the falls added to the eeriness of the situation. The horse evidently sensed that something was amiss, for it stumbled on the hill leading to the covered bridge. The "live corpse" chuckled to himself as he debated whether to spring his surprise on the bridge or wait until they hit the open fields further on. He decided in favor of the latter course.

The horse clattered over the bridge and climbed the slope toward Russia. The driver, totally unaware that his companion was full of life, spurred the animal to greater efforts.

When they hit the top of the first hill, the prankster in the blanket suddenly jabbed the driver in the ribs and said, "You stopped for a drink. How about giving me one?"

According to the prankster, the grave-robber jumped two feet in the air. All that could be seen of him was a pair of flapping coat-tails as he dashed madly across the fields.

The prankster did not pursue him, for not only had he retrieved the body, but he and his friend had acquired an excellent driving horse and a wagon.

BLACK HOLLOW

Youngsters who drive their "hotrods" to and from the Jones Bros. barn dance east of Remsen each Saturday night seldom realize that they dip through a hollow where Remsen's earliest murder was committed. If they did, maybe they would see the ghost of James Bull lurking in the woods.

Bull appeared in the village one evening in 1796, carrying with him a considerable sum of money with which he planned to purchase a lot in the Remsenburgh Patent. After eating supper with relatives, he started out on horseback. He rode through the dusk past Fairchild Corners and turned left near where Enlli Church now stands. In those days, the deep hollow that led toward denser wilderness was threaded by a narrow path which wound its way down into a dark, damp hollow crossed by a brook. Darkness had fallen when Bull rode into the hollow. In the morning, his body was found by a passerby, but the sum of money was gone.

Years later, a man on his death bed was said to have been overcome with remorse and confessed that he had murdered Bull and robbed him, but there is no record of the murderer ever having been brought to justice. The declivity in which Bull was slain is known to this da as Black Hollow.

Another tale involving a Negro is often tied to Black Hollow, but there seems to be no foundation for it, for the slaying took place in the area around Pen Y Graeg Chapel about fifty years later.

A Negro named William Johnson, then about 25 years old, had worked on farms in the Remsen and Steuben areas since his early childhood. Some accounts say that he or his family had been slaves of James Sheldon or Samuel Sizer, pioneer settlers, before their legal emancipation.

Johnson, commonly known as Black Bill, was a good man with an axe, so he was frequently employed to clear land for new settlers. Chester Kent needed men to fell some trees in his woodlot, so he engaged Black Bill, along with two other young men named Williams and Rowlands. All three were fond of liquor, so they brought along a bottle, which they emptied before they reached the lot. Once at work, some kind of argument developed, with the two white men taking sides against Johnson. Words led to fisticuffs. Williams and Rowlands pitched on Black Bill, beat him to death, and fled the country. Bill's body was found on the woodlot and was taken to Fairchild Cemetery and buried.

Those were the days when doctors needed cadavers for dissectional purposes, and usually got them by exhuming bodies of people who had recently died. Black Bill's body was lifted one dark night and carried away. Remsen, like Norway, had been troubled by ghouls for years, so fingers were pointed in the direction of the Fairchild Medical College. The men were gathering for a mass attack on the college when news leaked out that not Fairfield, but local doctors, had stolen Black Bill's corpse and had hidden it right in the village.

The village flew into an uproar. Ghost stories began to circulate, and every abandoned shack was considered a likely lurking place for the spirits of the murdered man. Evidently things began to get hot for the Remsen doctors, for they or someone brought Black Bill's body back to the cemetery and reburied it. In their haste, they failed fully to cover it.

A few days later, a respectable young lady from Remsen was walking through the cemetery toward dusk when she saw the hand of a corpse protruding through the dirt covering a grave. Thoroughly terrified, she let out a shriek and ran pell mell toward home, where she collapsed after reporting what she had seen in the cemetery.

Village condemnation fell upon the shoulders of the village authorities, who quieted the storm by sending out men with shovels to bury Black Bill properly.

The fact that the Negro had been buried in Fairchild Cemetery, which is relatively close to Black Hollow, gave rise to the belief that Black Bill was the man murdered in the hollow, and that the place got its name because Johnson was a Negro. If the "hotrodders" should ever slow down long enough to see a ghost in Black Hollow, I feel sure it will be the spirit of James Bull and not that of Black Bill Johnson.

ON TO PISECO!

Piseco Lake, now a popular resort, lay amid isolated wilderness a century ago. A trip to the lake constituted real adventure, as is testified by Ellis H. Roberts, editor of the *Utica Morning Herald,* who made a trek to the lake in September, 1855, together with General Richard U. Sherman and other sportsmen. Here is an excerpt from the story of their trip to Piseco (spelled Peseco by Roberts):

"Behold your scribe, together with those veterans of the forest, Gen. Sherman, Major Scholefield and Wm. B. Smith, mounted upon a wagon and, favored by the darkness, bidding adieu to the loved ones at home — and his exchanges and fault-finding patrons — and striking into the rural districts. Our wagon was a study for the painter; crammed and jammed with fishhooks and rods and guns—with creature comforts and utensils of cooking—with bedding and bread baskets—until the 'lofty pile' reached far above the wagon box and seat, and we were perforce compelled to "Lay around loose" upon the top, looking more like Mormon emigrants than the Christian citizens we were. I regret that I have no copy of our bill of fare at hand. Let it suffice to say that we had all the 'luxuries of the season' cozily packed in curious parcels and stowed away in divers boxes and baskets; parcels labeled 'Pork,' parcels labeled 'Pickles,' and parcels without any labels at all; strong meats for the hungry, knick-knacks for the fastidious, water for the thirsty. and cholera medicine for desperate emergencies. (Here this veracious chronicle compels me to scout the suspicion that we carried with us any definite number of 'original packages'—the party with the exception of the writer hereof being teetotalers of the most inveterate stripe.)

"Thus mounted, accoutred and provisioned, drawn by a blind mare and a balky horse, and our rear protected by a frying pan, a very large hound and a very small terrier, we plunged into the darkness and mud of Deerfield; awoke the echoes of the sleepy old 'Corners' by the rattling of our noisy vehicle; crawled slowly up the steeps of Deerfield Hills; plunged again into the woods beyond; blundered and groped our way through a couple of miles of the compactest darkness ever imported from Egypt; reined up opposite to what turned out to be a very well-kept tavern in a very vile-looking gulf—baited our nags and refreshed ourselves thereat; drove on through a miserable drizzle and over a very execrable road to Russia Corners; thence to some place not fit to name; thence into the woods where we tried to shoot a pigeon, and succeeded in losing one of our dogs and losing our own way in our efforts to recover him; thence to a wretched huddle by a strange misnomer called 'Ohio City,' inhabited principally by sand-hills, paralytic sheep and cadaverous poultry; thence into the woods so profoundly that all reckoning of furlongs, miles and leagues became hopelessly entangled in dead branches and mud holes; thence to the foot of a hill of such skiey altitude that the balky horse declared it was no use trying to scale it; and so doggedly reposed on his haunches, deaf to all sorts of physical arguments for the space of an hour; then over how many miles I shrink from reckoning, through woods, mud and darkness to a very rocky place called 'Morehouseville,' where we tarried till morning; thence ten miles through the woods and over a road so bad that we were not only obliged to carry ourselves with our own legs, but also, some of the distance, both horses and wagon, until we reached the southern shore of Lake Peseco. Here we sought the hospitality of a huntsman named COUCH, under whose roof we tarried during our sojourn.

"Peseco Lake once seen becomes a memory forever, enshrined among royal mountains whose crests, mirrored in its glassy bosom, look like huge, inverted castles; it works upon the eye and heart of the beholder with the potency of enchantment. Its waters, sparkling in the silver moonlight or glistening in the golden rays of the setting sun, are beautiful as a dream of Heaven. Stretching away to the northward, until its gleaming brightness is quenched in the shadow of the regal mountains beyond, and flanked on every side by the grandest and most glorious of forests, its quiet loveliness so strikingly contrasting with all around it, you involuntarily ask Why has this 'thing of beauty' been hidden away among these rugged wilds through all the serried centuries of the past?"

A COUPLE OF GINGERS

One of Uncle Jake Lewis' successors at the Remsen hotel continued the tradition of jolly good-fellowship that inimitable story-teller had established. Friend Bristol could not match Uncle Jake at spinning tall yarns, but he served better meals. It is said that Jake would get out in the road and ring a bell when he saw prospective customers approaching, and would bellow forth his menus of chicken, trout and steak dinners. Once inside, the customer might find himself facing a dish of baked beans and salt pork. Bristol, on the other hand, put on a good board, and often specialized in such delicacies as venison steaks and roast pheasant. On one occasion, when he received a gift of several birds from a hunter friend in the Middle West, he invited all his friends to a meal they never forgot.

Bristol ran a hotel in Remsen for about twelve years, together with his wife, Stella, who was a daughter of George Dawson, the Trenton hotel-keeper. He is remembered as a good-sized man, husky, smooth-shaven and good-looking. He liked fine horses, and his rig always attracted attention. He also took a keen interest in horse races, and acted as judge at the Trenton Agricultural Fair.

Hunters and fishermen loved Friend, for he was one of the first sportsmen to invade North Lake and other areas which then consisted of virgin forest. He came back from one fishing trip to North Lake with fifteen trout which weighed fifteen pounds after they had been dressed.

Bristol liked to share his hunting and fishing exploits with his customers. One evening, he was explaining how he and Eve Roberts had gone hunting that September day and had come back with eight birds, two of them larks. Gamekeeper Phelps, who was in the audience, found that Friend's remarks had put him on the spot, for a new game law had made the shooting of larks illegal before the first of October. Duty won over friendship in Phelps' mind, and he had Bristol and Roberts arrested for violating the game law. Bristol admitted having killed the larks, but he also claimed he knew nothing about the new law. Sportsmen and newspaper reporters rose to his defense, and he received countless letters wishing him luck. Phelps insisted that he had not really arrested his two friends, but had sued them for the penalty. Roberts and Bristol paid fines, and the case was closed.

Bristol built a camp on a little-known lake several miles east of Remsen. He spent considerable time and money fitting it up as a summer resort for himself, his family and his friends. He named it the Lake Julia Club after his daughter.

Being a hotel-keeper, Bristol did not believe in prohibition. One year, when the village of Remsen voted no license, he boarded up his wagon sheds and posted a sign, "No Admittance."

He co-operated after a fashion on election days and holidays, when village authorities asked him to close his bar. One year, when Remsen was in the midst of a rousing political campaign, a giant mass meeting was to be held, so Bristol and John (Bill L.) Williams, the two hotel-keepers, were asked to close up their bars.

A Remsen politician was much disturbed over this edict, so he went to Bristol and asked him what he should do if some influential reporter should want a drink of something more potent than water.

Bristol thought for a moment and said, "Ginger."

The politician ran into a Utica newspaperman who was dying for a drink, so the two men went over to the Bristol House. The password worked to perfection, and the scribe came out smiling.

About a quarter of an hour later, the reporter met a colleague who needed "whistle-wetting." They hurried to the Bristol House.

"We want a couple of gingers," said the first scribe knowingly.

Bristol eyed the pair and set up the drinks. The reporters gulped them down, made wry faces, paid and left. They collared the politician outside.

"Say," said the first scribe, "how'd you do it? You took me in to Friend, called for ginger and we got a little ginger and a big horn of whiskey. I took my friend here in and what did we get? A couple of gingers, pure and simple."

"Friend Bristol always believes in keeping a level head himself," replied the politician, "and he probably was doing you a kindness in helping you to do the same, especially during elections."

The Lake Julia Club went up in smoke about a year after Bristol's passing. The lake—well-stocked and prominently posted—causes trout fishermen to drool with envy.

BORROWED TRANSPORTATION

The Loomis gang from the Nine Mile Swamp did not operate extensively in the Adirondack foothills, but owners of horses had to be on the lookout for thieves who might "borrow" transportation and fail to return it.

A man from Watertown "found" a horse and buggy in Deerfield one Sunday in 1880 and decided to take a ride. Unfortunately, the rig belonged to Joseph Price, who trailed the thief to Holland Patent, where he enlisted the aid of T. J. Pooler, a former deputy sheriff of Herkimer County.

Price and Pooler caught up with the thief in Parker Hollow, halfway between Trenton and Prospect, where the Cincinnati Creek winds through a gorge. When Pooler tried to arrest the Watertown man, the latter broke from his grasp and ran for dear life toward the ravine, where he jumped forty feet into the chasm and disappeared. Pooler, unwilling to chance such a suicidal plunge, took a roundabout path to the creek, expecting to find a dead body on the rocks. Instead, he saw the Watertowner legging it toward Trenton. Pooler lit out after him, captured and handcuffed him, and took him to Holland Patent, where his wounds were dressed. It seems that the thief's fall had been broken by an overhanging limb. Pooler sent him packing to Deerfield to answer charges of stealing Price's horse and buggy.

Horses always seemed to turn up at points distant from their home barns. The watchman at Babbitt's foundry near the Erie Canal in Whitesboro found a foam-flecked mare dragging a wagon along the towpath around four o'clock one Sunday morning. It turned out that Charles Wolf, a farmer living a few miles out of Boonville, had returned from that village late the night before with his mare and wagon. Evidently the thief had wished to get to Whitesboro in a hurry, for he made the distance from Boonville to that place in about four hours. Wolf came to retrieve his property but the thief had "skedaddled."

Port Leyden also got into the act. The Rome police received a telegram from Daniel Douglass, who had heard that his stolen horse was in that city. They made a search, but no horse turned up. Deputy Mowers of the Port went to Rome with a description of the horse and the thief. Chief Farquharson of Rome spotted the man on a street and arrested him. The thief had no horse, but his pockets produced two watches and forty-five dollars. He admitted he had traded the horse for the watches and money at Hillside on the Black River Canal.

The continual hunt for horse thieves proved embarrassing for George E. Wood of New York, who drove through the foothills with a horse and buggy, selling pleating machines to housewives.

Wood pulled up before a Lowville hotel to refresh himself. A small crowd had gathered when he came out, and several men were examining his horse. Wood was not disturbed, for he was proud of his rig and liked to have folks admire it. He jumped into the buggy and clicked to the horse.

The men blocked his way, and one fellow began to ask Wood pointed questions about the horse and buggy. Wood's dander rose, and he was giving the man a piece of his mind when he discovered that his interrogator wore a constable's badge. The law officer produced a postal card describing a horse and buggy which had been stolen from Frank Harris of Watertown. Unfortunately for Wood, not only the horse and buggy, but he himself, fitted the description of the thief. The sheriff came along to reinforce the constable. Wood was arrested and spent the night in the Lowville lockup. Harris arrived the next morning to claim his property. He admitted that Wood's horse and buggy did not belong to him.

The following afternoon Wood landed in Boonville, where he drove to a farmhouse below the village to visit some customers. A pounding on the door revealed law officers from Boonville, armed with an identical postal card. Wood told what had transpired in Lowville, but the officers took him to Forestport and sent a telegram to Harris in Watertown before letting him go.

Several days later, Wood arrived in Canajoharie where, on the barn door, he found a poster with a description of Harris' horse and buggy. Wood went to the constable, explained what had happened in Lowville and Boonville, and begged not to be arrested again. When last seen, he was driving toward Saratoga, probably wondering where he would be picked up next.

SUMMER VISITORS

The Adirondack foothills, at the turn of the century, catered to an odd assortment of wanderers who made their way from farm to farm, doing a few odd jobs or merely accepting the hospitality of folks who felt sorry for them.

Mrs. Charles Smith of Stittville writes: "Old Alf Mowers was one of the delights of our childhood. In the early 1900's he was in the seventies, a little old man with bright blue eyes and a head of curls like a gone-to-seed dandelion. He would come trudging up the road, carrying a telescope bag hung with a dozen or more small packages, and carrying one or two big packages. I have always wondered what was in those bundles. Every summer he used to come to our house for a few days, and my mother never minded, as he was immaculately neat. Every day he would take a bar of laundry soap and head for the swimming hole. He always carried a sack of Little Falls diamonds, and if we kids teased him, he would threaten to disinherit us. (He was some undetermined relation to my grandmother.)

"Whenever Alf came, word would spread like wildfire through the neighborhood, and everyone able to walk or crawl would come to our house for an evening of singing, dancing and performing. Alf had a fine voice, and knew dozens, hundreds maybe, of folk songs, some in the old Palatine 'high Dutch' dialect. The old fellow would dance by the hour and almost kick our heads off. Many times I have thought that if Alf had been born seventy-five years later he might have gained fame and fortune instead of spending his old age in the County Home."

Mrs. Smith also remembers Bill Bala Williams, as does every elderly citizen of Remsen, for this bent Welshman with a withered limb which he called "the little arm," wandered from farm to farm each summer, singing for pennies. He would arrive with his worldly possessions wrapped in a red bandana handkerchief carried on a stick over his shoulder.

Bill Bala's chief claim to fame was the loudest voice ever heard in the foothills. His price for yelling was two cents and opinions vary as to whether he could be heard two or four miles away, depending on the clearness of the atmosphere and the veracity of the teller. He liked to sing hymns, either in the streets or in Peniel Church, where his booming tones carried above the voices of the congregation.

Bill was not neat like Alf Mowers, and one farmer's wife used to serve him tea and bread in the yard, for she did not want her house infested, but most people took him in, sometimes for weeks.

He liked to stop with Tom Richards up near Pen Y Graeg chapel. Tom always welcomed him, but cautioned him about disturbing the neighbors, warning him that John Hughes, a big Welshman who had moved onto a farm a mile away, would shake him if he yelled.

Bill was practicing a few salvos one morning when he saw Hughes striding down the road. Bill cringed with fright. "What shall I do?" he asked Richards. "Where is it I can go?"

Richard's eyes twinkled. He decided to teach the old yeller a lesson, so he said, "Run, you. Hide in the haymow in the barn."

When Hughes came up to pass the time of day, Richards told him what he had said to Bill, so the visitor decided to go through with his part of the game. He pulled Bill out of the haymow, held him at arms' length, and threatened to shake him until his teeth chattered.

Bill Bala kept his voice under control while on the Richards farm, but he made up for lost time in Remsen, where he roamed the streets and sang for a penny—or was it two pennies?—and usually carried a pocketful of coppers back to the County Home.

Prospect's most famous summer visitor was Sam Hemstreet, a badly crippled old fellow who walked with the aid of two canes. He stopped with Henry Hagedorn, the miller in the Basin, but would manage to get up to the village each day, where he would sit quietly in Chan Hodge's store until someone would bring up his pet project. Sam's eyes would light up and his voice would gain strength as he would tell how, during the War of 1812, some troops had crossed over Boon's Bridge and had dropped a cannon into the deep hole in the West Canada Creek directly below the bridge.

Prospect folks took little stock in Sam's story, but with the damming of the creek by the Niagara Mohawk Power Corporation, some present residents might be surprised if Sam's cannon is found.

THE TANTALIZING TRAMP

Spring forty-odd years ago meant more than pussy-willows and flooded streams, for that was the season when the tantalizing tramp emerged from hiberation and wandered from village to village, seeking anything but honest labor.

These tramps were a picturesque lot, particularly in their careless manner of dress. Water did not interest them, either for drinking or for bathing, and the razor was virtually unknown. Their clothing consisted of odd assortments of hand-me-downs, frequently patched with unmatching colors, much like the dress the clown, Emmett Kelly, uses to entertain audiences.

Tramps literally swamped Boonville the year that village built its water works. A few of them provided amusement for the villagers. A gay and festive tramp named Willie McGuire had imbibed enough of the "elixir of life" to be funny, so he danced and sang and boasted of conquering the world until an unsympathetic constable put him in the lockup to cool off. One lady asked a tramp why there were so many wanderers on the road. "We are looking for work and praying we won't get it," he replied. The lady gave him breakfast and escorted him to the woodpile. A short time later, she found there, not the tramp, but a note which read: "Tell them you saw me but did not see me saw the wood."

Lyons Falls was infested with tramps. One tantalizing fellow came to the door and asked the housewife, "Couldn't you fix it up so I could have a cup of tea or coffee?" When she refused, he grinned and said, "Yes, tramps are plenty. The rich made 'em, and you can't classify 'em. There is as much difference in 'em as there is in women."

While some of the tramps provided humor and philosophy, many were bad actors. Constable Cramer of Boonville could not keep up with them. Tramps attempted to hold up W. W. Finlayson near Erwin Park, but he drove them away. A man stepped out of the darkness and tried to grasp the bridle of Ole Ward's horse. One tough-looking fellow entered the store of Mrs. Nicholas Schweinsberg in broad daylight. The lady told him to get out, which he refused to do until he could get some "goodies." He had underestimated his hostess, for Mrs. Schweinsberg chased him out with a stick of wood. Three tramps appeared at the house of William Bowen and brazenly demanded lodging for the night. News got around that Bowen had driven his "guests" away with a revolver, so the sale of firearms rose appreciably in Boonville.

Remsen also had its troubles. John W. Thomas, the poormaster, was hounded by knights of the road. One night he heard someone pass around his house, so he got up, thinking it another charity patient. He heard a window being raised, whereupon his wife let out a shriek. "Go away!" The tramp obeyed, but Thomas said afterward that he would have put an extra hole in the thief's face if he had caught him.

The outlying farms were choice bait for tramps. John Jones and his wife were planning to attend a wedding in Remsen the next day, so John's best suit had been brushed and laid out for the event. A tramp came to the door and asked for lodgings. Mrs. Jones took him in. The next morning, Jones' suit had disappeared with the tramp. The hired man on Dave Jones' farm in Steuben met a tramp at the door and told him that the family was away. The tramp swore that he would get into the house, whereupon the hired man went at him and received for his pains a black eye and a few bruises after having been knocked down. He reached for his watch. It was gone, along with the tramp.

Tramps did not always come out on top in these affairs. Owen Roberts, a farmer who lived two miles north of Trenton on the road to Remsen, was awakened at three in the morning by the sound of breaking glass. He rushed to the sitting room, where he encountered a burly tramp. Though the farmer weighed but 120 pounds, he grabbed an unloaded shotgun and bounced it over the intruder's head, knocking him cold. Mrs. Roberts picked up her new telephone and called the deputy sheriff, who came and arrested the intruder.

A Lowville farmer, A. C. Eaton, had a more primitive way of handling tramps. He hired two and gave them comfortable clothes. They ran away, whereupon Eaton took after them in his horse and buggy and caught them near Boonville, where he took away their clothes and left them "in that picturesque costume which Adam and Eve wore in the Garden of Eden."

II. STREAMS

The swift, brown streams ran coursing toward the sea,
Their amber flecked and whitened with the foam;
And mighty logs, torn from their forest home,
Came hurtling down the springtide, strong and free,
To pile like jackstraws in a wooden dome,
While lumberjacks, with peaveys, calks and grit,
Untangled the great timbers bit by bit
And sent them thund'ring toward their sawmill boom.

The foothills rivers ring no more with cries.
"He's in!" no longer grips the hearts of men.
Nor will the barkeeps ever hear again
The songs and jests and stories tinged with lies.
For those brave men, survivors of the streams,
These folklore tales may reconstruct some dreams.

"WHOO-EE-EE! THE PUSSY-WILLOW!"

States, in choosing flowers to represent them, usually favor roses, laurel or some other striking blossom. The riverjacks in the Adirondack foothills gave their allegiance to the pussy-willow, for it meant that the ice had broken in the creeks and rivers; that the log drive was about to begin.

"Hi-yee! Who-ee-ee!"

The cry would rise from the leathery lungs of the first jack to discover a pussy-willow in bloom. He would break off a few budded branches, show them to his pals and ask, "Ain't this the damndest, purtiest, little posy you ever did see?"

At this harbinger of spring, the bunkhouses would seethe with activity. Calks on leather boots would be tested for sharpness. Peaveys and pikepoles were checked for strength. Laughs and joyful cries would ring through the building, and tall stories of other drives would rise easily to the lips of the jacks.

The eyes of the bosses also brightened at the sight of the first pussy-willow. If a hall of fame is ever established, Dan McCauley, Sol Carnahan, Jim McBeth, Tim Dunn, Henry Kreuzer, Jim Hill, George Abbott, and John B. Todd would become charter members, for they were the great men of the rivers, familiar with the "raw right-angled jam," the "wing jam," and the "key log." They had a flair for handling not only logs but men, from the stolid "pig-yokers" who worked near shore to the flashy, temperamental riverjacks who risked life and limb in order to break jams and get the logs down the amber streams to the mills.

The river boss had a ticklish and responsible job, for he had to "high-spot" the drive; that is, he had to decide when the wind and the water level were right to send the logs down the streams. The trick was to turn the logs into the streams a few at a time, in order to prevent them from hanging up on rocks or other obstacles and thus cause a jam.

Early drives were run on the spring freshets, but later, water was impounded near the heads of streams and released at the proper time. Any miscalculation might result in either a waste of water or in catching the riverjacks before they were prepared to handle the mass of logs.

The spring drive usually lasted two to three weeks, depending on the weather. "Pig-yokers," armed with long pikepoles, guarded the banks, particularly inlets where "wing jams" might develop. Using their poles, they guided logs along the streams, rather than let them collect near the shore.

Riverjacks, clad in multi-colored shirts and jackets, "stagged" pants and calked shoes, worked in the streams, guiding "ornery" logs with their peaveys, or dancing from log to log with the agility of cats. In the early days in the foothills, most of the riverjacks were from Maine, New Brunswick or Quebec, and some came over from the Raquette and Hudson Rivers. The French-speaking "Canucks" added many a choice word to vocabularies already rich with profanity.

Jams annoyed the river bosses and lent zest to the lives of the jacks. To the former, they meant "back-snys" and "plugs" which delayed the drive; to the latter, they spoke of the excitement of breaking a jam and riding logs on the streams.

Once the "key logs" had been pulled, either with peaveys or with dynamite, and the logs began to slip in all directions, the riverjack was in his element. He was a picturesque figure as he danced from log to log or paddled toward shore on a twisting piece of timber with only a peavey for an oar and a rudder. Many a jack "washed his clothes" before reaching shore, and not a few never made it.

"Sacking up the rear" to get the remaining logs downstream after the main drive had gone through was usually done in North River boats by a mop-up squad, while the jacks hied themselves off to a tavern to celebrate.

Forestport, Hinckley, Prospect, Port Leyden and Lyons Falls usually bore the brunt of these revelries, though jacks who couldn't wait that long might light up Seth Lyons' place above Forestport or Bill Wright's in Wilmurt.

The departure of the river men always attracted the attention of folks in the villages. In April, 1891, when Forestport was suffering from a fire which had destroyed 25 buildings, the correspondent to the *Boonville Herald* found time to note: "It was a novel sight last Monday evening to see the wagon loads of drivers for the woods going to the railroad station on their way home. They were a happy crowd, singing, shouting and offering treats out of their black bottles. There were probably 50 or 60 of them, mostly Canadians."

THE FABULOUS CARNAHANS

Sol Carnahan came down from New Brunswick in the early eighteen-nineties to take charge of a log drive on the West Canada Creek. He was so homesick at first that he refused to answer letters from his relatives for fear that they would write back to him. He felt more at home when his wife and his two younger brothers, Ab and Erv, joined him in Wilmurt.

Sol conducted drives down the West Canada Creek and the Black and Moose Rivers for years. No river boss ever gained more respect from his men. When Sol retired to finish out his years on a farm near Cooperstown, the riverjacks and pig-yokers sensed that they had lost their dearest friend.

Sol knew his job from A to Z. In his younger days, he was so good at driving logs that he was rewarded with the highest praise given to a man in his profession—the name of "bubble-walker." Though Sol could not swim a stroke, he probably took more chances than any riverjack in the foothills. To celebrate one Fourth of July at Bellingertown, he rode through the white water of a flooded Black River with his peavey held straight up before him, and sailed under the bridge to the applause of a group of rivermen who had gathered to see his performance.

No foreman in the woods ever worked men harder than did Sol Carnahan, yet he won and held the admiration of them all. During the drive, he arose at three in the morning and rousted out his help. Sol's men complained that they never saw daylight. One fellow claimed that when he went to bed he hung up his pants on the bedpost and they were still swinging when Sol woke him in the morning.

The men worked hard for Sol, for he paid better wages than did most jobbers, and food was plentiful. When the drive neared Northwood, Will Light used to come over from his hotel with steaming food which he served right on the shore of the creek. It is said that one hungry riverjack, smelling the food, forgot to ride the logs, but merely dove in and swam across the icy creek.

Sol also knew how to relax with his men. Trume Brown, who worked for Sol as a young lad and for years afterward, used to say that

Carnahan was a bad actor when in the cups. Sol didn't get disagreeable, but he let himself go with such wild abandon that he was the scourge of hotel keepers from Utica to Piseco, though they tolerated his shenanigans because he was such a good spender. On one occasion, when he and his jacks were drinking at the Bucket of Blood in Utica, Sol asked the proprietor casually, "What will you take for your damned bar, just for an hour?" The canny proprietor set the price at five hundred dollars, whereupon Sol produced a roll of greenbacks that would have choked a cow, peeled off five hundred-dollar bills and tossed them on the bar. Again, at the Mansion House, Sol spotted a piano and felt in the mood for singing shanties. Since neither he nor any of his men could play, he jumped up on the piano and pounded the keys with his boots, all the while roaring, "The Jam on Garry's Rock." When the hotel man protested that Sol had wrecked the piano, which was true, Sol sent his men to a music store and bought a new one. The proprietor tried to remove the old, battered instrument, but Sol cried, "That's mine," and continued to play with his feet and sing shanties until he almost dropped from exhaustion.

Sol's most dramatic exploit occurred in Foote's Hotel in Piseco, where lumberjacks were celebrating the culmination of a successful drive. Everyone seemed to be there but Sol, and the party was getting duller by the minute. Suddenly, without warning, the door burst open and Sol rode in on horseback, pranced up to the bar, and had his drinks while the bartender patted the horse's nose.

Though Sol "palled around" with his men, he stood for no foolishness from them while on the job. If the creek was ready for the drive, he would send word to the Utica hotels that he would meet his men at Prospect station with buckboards at a certain time. The men always showed up so that Bill Hughes and Morey Platt could drive them from the station to the woods.

Tote-drivers were sent out frequently for supplies, and Jack Roberts, a burly fellow, usually got the assignment. Trume Brown used to tell how he and three other young fellows were delegated to go with Roberts to pick up a load of supplies which included a barrel of whiskey. On the way back, the men thought it would do no harm to tap the barrel and have a little drink. The pleasure proved so habit-forming that they lost all sense of time and direction. Three days later, they appeared at Sol's camp, minus most of the whiskey. Sol resorted to quick justice. Inasmuch as the barrel of whiskey had cost $125, he took $25 from the wages of each of the five men, amounts which constituted a whole month's earnings.

Sol fitted in well with the natives up around Wilmurt, where he ran a store. At a donation for the minister held in the Eureka House, he donned a white apron and served the guests. Folks up that way say no waiter at the Waldorf-Astoria could have done a better job than the river boss did on that occasion.

Sol's younger brothers, Adam, commonly called Ab, then about twenty years old, and Erv, a year or so younger, joined Sol in Wilmurt, and their coming did much to settle his early discontent. They worked with Sol on drives and gave promise of developing into superior riverjacks. Ab, in particular, was becoming "the best river man who ever looked at the creek." Erv would have made better progress if he could have stayed away from liquor. He kept a bottle under his bed and would start each day by taking a big swig of whiskey and eat his breakfast for a chaser.

Two years after the brothers came to Wilmurt, Sol was conducting the Trenton Falls Lumber Company's spring drive near Jock's Lake outlet. The creek was at flood peak, a boiling, seething mass of brown water. A dangerous jam developed, so Ab took Dan Pinney and a boatman and rode to the head of the jam, where he and Dan jumped onto the logs while the boatman remained ready to take them to shore when the jam broke. The two riverjacks went to work with their peaveys and succeeded in loosening logs near a big rock. The jam began to move before they could get back to the boat, and the creek became filled with dancing, tumbling logs. Ab and Dan jumped from log to log to get as near shore as possible. Seeing open water ahead, they each selected a log and began to ride it, paddling and pushing toward shore with their peaveys. Ab made out well, but Pinney was being drawn toward rapids which led to a waterfall no man had ever ridden successfully. Ab, seeing his pal's predicament, deliberately placed his peavey against Dan's log and sent it toward shore. The force of the shove sent Ab's log back into the stream, but he paddled back and gave Dan's log another push. Pinney jumped from his log and swam to the shore and safety. Not so Carnahan. His log was caught by the swirling water. With great skill, he "cuffed" the log into position and faced the white water ahead. He might have ridden to safety, but the log struck a submerged rock. He was thrown far ahead into the roaring stream. Pinney saw him rise to the surface only to be crushed to death between two colliding logs. His body was recovered hours later far down the creek. Sol took it to New Brunswick for burial. Ab Carnahan, at the age of twenty-two, had given his life to save that of another man.

Erv stayed on with Sol. Like Ab, he was a soft-spoken, intelligent lad who did many errands for his elder brother, for his drinking habits had eliminated him from work on the rivers. Sol was driving logs up in the Moose River country one spring and Erv was sent to Utica for the payroll money. Muggins Laird wanted to go along, though Erv and Sol both knew Muggins would kill a man to get a drink of liquor. Sol waited patiently for payroll money that never arrived. Erv and Muggins were seen getting off the train and starting toward the Carnahan lumber camp. That was the last anyone ever saw of Erv Carnahan.

Old timers say that fingers of suspicion were pointed at Muggins, who seems to have won the dislike of all the jacks, but nothing could ever be proved. Eph Wheeler, who knew Sol well in the old days, said that he met Sol in a Utica hotel a few years before the riverman's death. He asked Sol if he ever had had any word from Erv, whereupon Sol shook his head sadly.

The Carnahans have become more or less of a legend along the West Canada Creek. The few men left who once worked for Sol will always say, "Sol Carnahan? He was a great old Sol."

RIDING WITH DEATH

Each spring, hundreds of young riverjacks rode with death on the West Canada Creek and the Moose and Black Rivers. Dressed in gaily checkered shirts, "stagged" pants, and boots studded with calks, they danced from log to log, plying their peaveys to loosen single logs and thus break jams, or "burled" down a stream on a rolling log with footwork that would have made a ballerina envious.

Prominent among these riverjacks was a slender, agile native of Port Leyden. Gene McBeth had ridden rivers successfully for years, so he laughed off any thought that he might be a victim of a breaking jam.

McBeth came up from Utica one spring to superintend a drive on Mill Creek, which empties into the West Canada at Nobleboro. Tim Dunn, the jobber, had built a dam on the upper stillwater to hold back the water so it could be released at one time and thus carry 10,000 logs down to the West Canada and on to Hinckley.

Mill Creek in the spring tumbles over granite rocks "big as a log shack" as it rushes and roars downhill to the West Canada. It is not a stream built for log riding, for it sweeps through a narrow gorge filled with cascades. Here a "wing jam" had piled up on a great boulder near the shore.

McBeth, never a man to leave a dangerous job to others, took two men to loosen the jam before Dunn released the water above and let the thousands of other logs rush down the gorge. While the riverjacks were plying their peaveys, the key log unexpectedly let loose and the whole jam leaped forward.

The three expert riverjacks ran toward the head of the jam. McBeth, in the lead, was leaping nimbly from log to log when he noticed that his companions were not with him, so he waited for them to catch up and saw to it that they both jumped safely into the water and struck out for shore. When his time to jump came, it was too late!

Gene had only one slim chance; to ride the tumbling mass of logs downstream and hope he could reach the West Canada safely. With his peavey held horizontally in front of his body, the young athlete put on the greatest exhibition of log-riding the jacks who ran along the shore had ever seen. He leaped high in the air to another log in an effort to reach shore. He avoided swinging logs with agile twists of his legs. One crashing of logs sent him to his knees, but he was up again, balancing himself nimbly on a twisting log. The last the men saw of Gene McBeth before he rounded a bend in the creek was an agile, death-defying riverjack, now riding, now balancing, now leaping from log to log, ever trying to get to a shore he would never reach. His body was found a week later. Every bone had been broken, but strange to relate, not even a bruise marred his handsome face.

Three men came to the West Canada Creek from Thurman in Warren County to work on a drive superintended by Colonel E. H. Talbot, a Civil War veteran who was almost as well-known in logging circles as was Sol Carnahan. James D. (Bud) Smith, a 39-year-old bachelor, was a veteran of many a drive, while his cousin, Herb Smith, and his friend, Truman Brown, were youngsters breaking in their eye-teeth on swirling logs.

A bad jam developed below Indian River, so a large group of men went out to loosen the logs. The river was at its flood, and a large amount of bark and other debris had crept in between the logs and had loosened them prematurely. Talbot yelled a warning and the men scurried for shore. Trume Brown used to say, "That there jam went straight up in the air like a mountain. I landed halfway up a tree on the shore, right up in the branches. Bud fell between a couple of logs and got crushed." Herb Smith, seeing his cousin's predicament, danced across the crashing logs, got his arms under the injured man's shoulders, and dragged him to the shore. Afterward, Herb was appalled at the extent of his feat. Bud was taken to the Barborn House, a "rum shack" three miles above Nobleboro, and a doctor came to see him, but Bud's body had been so badly crushed that he died the next day.

On another occasion, Talbot was driving logs down the Black River below Bellingertown, where the river dips and races over shelves of rock. Pig-yokers were working along the edge of a jam, while Bing Carnright, Eph Wheeler and Frank Huckabone went out on the logs. Talbot suddenly yelled the warning that the jam was breaking. Wheeler, then a sixteen-year-old who was "quicker than a paper devil," started upstream. So did Huckabone. Wheeler, looking back, saw Bing run downstream on he logs. This was bad, for Carnright not only had poor eyesight and wore glasses, but he was a novice at driving. Eph saw Bing disappear between two logs just before he jumped into fifteen feet of water and struck out for shore and safety. At the inquest, he and Huckabone were scared out of their wits, not because they were guilty of any misdemeanor, but because Coroner J. Wallace Douglass of Boonville had such a frightening beard.

The Moose River also had its share of tragedy, but the one that touched folks in Port Leyden was the death of young Cless Brown, who left a young wife behind. Cless was one of the best drivers for the Gould Paper Company, so the task of picking out the key log from a jam near Sliding Rock was assigned to him. Cless did his job fearlessly and well. When the jam broke, he jumped onto a detached log with the idea of riding it to shore. Much to his horror, the log swung abruptly toward midstream. The channel ahead was filled with black rocks hidden by the rushing water. Cless knew they were there, and tried to avoid them, but his log, running at break-neck speed, struck one of the rocks. Cless was thrown high into the air, but he managed to land on his feet. His log had been reversed by the collision, but Cless pivoted neatly so he could face the dangers ahead. Peavey in hand, the young riverjack rode bravely down the river. Men cheering him from the shore felt sure he would ride to safety when, without warning, another log struck Brown's log from the rear. Their ends met in a violent crash. Brown's peavey flew from his hands and his body hurtled over his log, disappeared into the rushing torrent and was sucked under the jam.

Despite tragedies, the gay riverjacks in their checkered shirts came back year after year. For them, it was a way of life.

THE DOD BLIMPED STERK

During the logging days on the West Canada Creek, there lived at Seaberry Settlement a family which used to settle for at least one or two additions a year. Including two sets of twins, the children numbered eleven, though the three oldest boys were scarcely out of knee-breeches. Like all boys, they resented the chore of "minding baby" while their mother prepared meals or did the family washing. When they got wind of another approaching arrival, they decided to do something about it.

The doctor arrived to discover Luke, Willie and Sam anxiously scanning the sky. Luke kept both hands on his .22 rifle, Willie had his air-gun against his shoulder, while Sam was putting ammunition into his bean-shooter.

"What's going on, boys?" the doctor asked.

"You'll see," said Luke. "We'll get him this time sure."

"Get what?"

"Never mind. We'll get him sure." Luke and his brothers turned away and concentrated on the sky.

They were sitting in a row when the doctor emerged from the house. "Well, boys," he asked, "what are you hunting?"

"We've been layin' for that dod blimped sterk," said Luke. "I guess we fixed him this time all right."

"You did?" laughed the doctor. "You're too late. You didn't watch sharp enough. He sneaked down the chimney and brought twins."

"Ain't that just our luck?" moaned Luke. "Yes'day I lost a woodchuck and today—" He headed for the woods, followed by his equally dejected brothers.

THRILLING RESCUES

One afternoon in May, 1909, Mrs. Lowell Odit was hanging up clothes behind her home overlooking Wilmurt Falls on the West Canada when she heard a cry for help rise above the roar of the creek. Looking upstream, she saw a man riding a log. As she watched the log rolled and threw its rider into the water. He rose to the surface and clutched the end of the log.

"Low!" Mrs. Odit cried to her husband, "there's a man in the creek above the falls. He'll go over them for sure."

Low rushed to his wife's side as the man cried, "Goodbye. I got to go!" and was carried over the falls into the pond which backed up water for Richards' mill. The Odits gasped in amazement, for Wilmurt Falls had always been considered a death trap, but the log had picked the one course possible to get the man through. The danger was far from over, for a second fall at the mill dam would undoubtedly prove fatal.

"It's Muggins Laird," gasped Low. "He ain't no swimmer." He carried a long board to the creek's edge and stretched out on his stomach on an overhanging hemlock where he could push the board within reach of the man in the water.

"Swim a little, Muggins," cried Low.

"I can't. I'm all numb and can't move."

Odit coaxed Muggins' log with his board and drew it toward him until he could get a hold on Muggins' shirt. Slowly, but surely, he got Muggins to shore and to the house, where the riverjack warmed himself, had a cup of strong coffee, and marched back up the river in his wet clothes, thankful that he had received no more than a bad ducking.

Rivermen wore heavy woollens, so they were not afraid of a spill into the water. Nor did the fact that many of them could not swim a stroke deter them from taking chances with dangerous rapids. The men were joking with George Dolly, a husky, two-hundred-pounder who had little skill with the peavey and was unable to swim. Dolly, tired of the joshing, bet the others ten dollars he could get down through a particularly rough stretch of "white water" unscathed. The men tried to dissuade Dolly, but they covered his money.

Dolly picked up a peavey and jumped onto a log, which he pushed toward the rapids. He lasted one split second. Soon he was thrashing around like a walrus as the current carried him downstream. Watchers along the shore could see first an arm, then a leg and occasionally Dolly's head. They felt sure the big fellow was riding to his death. Dolly had other ideas. He eddied around in the swirling water and rolled and tumbled to shore to receive his ten dollars.

One of the most daring river rescues took place near the bridge at McKeever in April, 1914. John B. Todd, superintendent of the Gould Paper Company drive, had already saved one man from going over a fall below the bridge by throwing him a rope and drawing him to the boom above the fall. His boss riverman, Jim Haley, was destined to perform a greater miracle.

Heavy rains had caused logs to jam against the McKeever bridge piers. More logs tumbled against them, with the result that the jam resembled a huge game of jackstraws with the Moose River racing beneath it. Riverjacks were sent out with peaveys to loosen some logs from the mass and send them into the rushing current.

When the jam broke with a roar, Jack McGee, a green hand, was unable to leave the logs. The other jacks saw his peril and yelled for him to run up the jam. Instead, he became panic-stricken and did nothing.

Jim Haley, who was standing on the bridge, yelled for McGee to lie down on the logs, with the hope that he would pass under the bridge safely. McGee chose one log instead of two or three. He was swept under the bridge and into the river.

Haley heard the cry, "He's in!" He grabbed a peavey, leaped from the bridge to a dancing log, dug his "corks" in, balanced himself, and jumped from log to log in McGee's direction. When he had overtaken the drowning man, Haley sank his peavey into his log, braced himself, and drew McGee out of the water. Holding the almost unconscious man over his knees, he directed the log to shore and safety.

COURT GOT A CHASER

Up Morehouseville way lived Henry Kreuzer, who not only was a key figure in the logging industry, but who also ran a hotel frequented by lumberjacks. It is said that Kreuzer made whiskey by the washtubful and threw in a plug of tobacco to color it.

Kreuzer had business at the county seat in Lake Pleasant one day, so he left the bar in charge of his nephew, Henry Rickard, a peace-loving man who seldom drank.

Rickard got along famously until Courtney Tetro walked in. This big fellow had a county-wide reputation as a bully.

"Give me a drink," growled Court. "Give me another drink. Give me a quart."

Rickard went to the back room to get a quart bottle, but he kept an eye on Court and saw the big fellow snatch a quart from the bar and carry it outside.

Court was back at the bar when Rickard came with the bottle. "Charge me with two drinks and a quart," said Court.

"What about the quart you stole?" asked Rickard.

Court rose up in righteous indignation. "Why, you little snot," he screamed, "don't tell me I stole anything."

Rickard stood his ground. "You sure did," he said, "I saw you."

Court made a swipe at Rickard, who parried the blow and proceeded to give the bully the most artistic thrashing he had ever received.

Kreuzer returned to find Court sitting outside, nursing numerous cuts and a black eye.

"Why," gasped Kreuzer, "what happened, Court?"

Court grinned wryly, put a hand to his eye and replied, "This is what your new bartender gave me for a chaser."

THE GHOST OF THE KUYAHOORA

There lived, as I've heard say, near the running water,
An old man and his wife, who had a beauteous daughter,
Right loving, fond and true, a young man loved her dearly.
They often rambled there through groves and fields of barley.
Says Kate, "I'll take the water pail and get a pail of water."
And musing as she went she thought upon her daughter.
Her old man Joe was there to realize his wishes
With rod and line and fly a catching little fishes.
Quite tranquil in his mind upon the bank there lying,
He turned his head behind and saw his old wife crying.
"Now what's the matter, Kate, what is the matter, woman?
What's running through your pate, 'tis something more than common?"
"Oh, Joe," poor Kate replied, "I have a troubled fancy.
I heard the waters roar and thought upon our Nancy.
If Tom and Nan should wed and such a thing there may be,
The marriage may bring forth a pretty little baby.
And when the baby walks and just begins to toddle,
Perhaps it may come here and in these waters paddle."
"Yes, Kate, 'tis very true the baby may be drowned,
And cast upon the shore and afterwards be found,
And buried it would be, that's a common after dying.
Oh, pretty, sweet baby—" and then began a crying.
Perhaps it might be fate that brought these lovers walking,
And heard old Joe and Kate a crying in their talking.
They asked the reason what and why—for they did cry so,
Then all together bawled that such a babe should die so.
They sat upon the green while Katie told the tale, oh!
No tongue hath heard or seen how they did weep and wail, oh!
They all went crying home; Tom, old man, wife and daughter,
Each night the ghost doth come and wail upon the water.

*This crude poem from the Wilmurt country, as recalled by the late C. B. Hodge of Prospect in 1901, shows the fear of the West Canada Creek in the hearts of the natives.

III. SAWMILLS

There was a time when gang saws sang and whined,
And piles of chips sent flavor toward the sun
In Forestport and Hinckley. And the fun
Of drinking at the tavern bars combined
With fisticuffs and brawls when day was done.
And lumberjacks, while waiting for the drive,
Would wrestle in the streets, and strain and strive
Till one man sat on top, the battle won.

And once a week, on Saturdays at two,
The baseball teams would battle tooth and nail,
While fans would press against the rustic rail
To cheer the home team on, the foe to boo.
Each vict'ry called for celebration toasts.
Defeats were drowned in alcoholic boasts.

SEA SERPENT?

A Kickapoo medicine show played Forestport in June, 1893, and folks liked it so well that it stayed two weeks. The small boys of the village were attracted to the two sons of the manager. One of them, a lad of fifteen, liked to show off his prowess as a knife-thrower and rifle-shot, and his skill with these weapons gained him the hero-worship of a group of ten-year-olds. When he suggested to one of the boys that they build a raft and float it on McGuire's Pond, the Forestport youngster responded with a will, so the pair spent days constructing the raft, which they navigated on the pond with a long pole.

Other Forestport boys became fascinated by the raft, so they coaxed the favored one to let them try it. The Indian boy came to the pond one day and found that the raft had not been moored properly, so he brandished a stick at his new-found friend and said, "If you touch that raft again, I'll hit you with this stick."

Despite this warning, three boys decided to take one more ride. They doffed their clothes and pushed the raft a respectable distance from shore, for they were beginners at the art of swimming and did not want to get into deep water. They were having a merry time, shouting to each other and digging the pole into the bottom in order to propel the raft, when they became aware of a louder noice from the shore. Looking up, they discovered men, women and children running toward the pond. They jumped into the water to cover their nakedness.

"Come out of there!" a man cried. "Don't you know there's a sea serpent in the pond?"

The boys didn't know it, but they preferred death at the hands of a sea serpent to exposure of their bodies before all of Forestport, so they ducked under until the water came up to their chins.

The crowd on shore became frantic. Mothers, fathers, brothers and sisters coaxed and pleaded, but the boys refused to come to shore. Finally, an older boy who had gone swimming with the trio on numerous occasions, managed to coax them, red-faced and shivering, to the shore, where they jumped into their clothes without drying off their bodies.

The commotion had started that morning, when a man passing McGuire's Pond reported that he had seen an animal with the head of a horse and the body of a fish rise up through the tanbark and sawdust which floated in patches on the surface.

Folks had scoffed at this report, but they sat up and took notice when three other versions of the phenomena were reported. One claimed that the animal spouted water and was at least a whale; the second contended that the animal could be a sea lion; the third, which described the thing as a sea serpent of stupendous proportions, caused considerable alarm in the village.

Women stopped their washing—it was a Monday—and men grabbed their rifles and shotguns. Children ran whooping through the streets on their way to McGuire's Pond. So, when the unsuspecting boys looked to the shore, a veritable army was assembling to take care of the horse-fish, whale, sea lion or sea serpent, whichever it might be.

The shivering boys, ashamed at their exposure, lurked near the edge of the crowd awaiting developments. No one was disappointed. The water on McGuire's Pond began to move, slowly at first and then more rapidly, and a great, brown body rose, floated for a few minutes, then separated and sank beneath the surface. The phenomenon was repeated three times before the eyes of the astonished spectators, and all kinds of theories were advanced as to the nature of the beast and the reason for its appearance.

The leaders of the village did not enter into these conjectures. They decided that the "serpent" was but a body of tanbark or sawdust which either by gases or some other source had been raised to the surface. To satisfy the people, they had the pond drained that evening. No serpent was found.

Some folks died hard, however, and a series of campfires dotted the shores of the pond that night, tended by armed men who felt sure that the serpent would reappear. It didn't.

One of the boys who had been on the raft still thinks that the continuous poling stirred up the quantity of tanbark which used to drift down every year from the tannery on Woodhull Creek and settle at the bottom of McGuire's Pond.

The Kickapoo boy probably attributed the "miracle" to Indian medicine.

SABBATH IN HINCKLEY

Tim Healey, bartender at Mike Ryan's Empire House, perched on a desk with his feet resting on a chair. Hinckley showed signs of calming down as the weekend drew to a close. Only the voice of an occasional drunk on the main street and the strains of an accordion from Little Italy carried to Tim's ears. He looked up at the clock. Ten-thirty. He wished Mike would give the sign to close up.

He cocked an ear. The approaching strains of *Marching Through Georgia* drifted through the opened door, emphasized by the pounding of boots. Fluctuations in pitch told Tim all he needed to know. A gang from the sawmill had decided to light up the village on this Sabbath night. Tim was no man to dodge a scrap, but he hoped the marchers would choose one of the other three hotels for their celebration.

He was doomed to disappointment. A dozen huskies from the sawmill marched through the door, two abreast. Each man shouldered a piece of edging. At the head strode Alex Burns, who could be a tough customer. "Halt!" cried Burns. The little army broke ranks and dove for the barroom. "We want a drink and be quick about it," Burns shouted to Healey.

"Not tonight," said Tim. "Mike's orders."

"Good old Mike won't give us a drink?" asked Burns in mock astonishment. "Come on, boys, let's give three cheers for Mike." He pulled the chair from beneath Tim's feet.

Tim moved quicker than a cat. He wrestled the chair out of Alex's hands and swung it at the leader's head.

This gesture touched off a riot. Edgings flailed around the barroom, belaboring the heads and backs of friend and foe. Loud curses mingled with shrieks of pain.

Suddenly, apparently from nowhere, appeared the proprietor, Mike Ryan. He was swinging an axe with both hands. "Get out of my hotel," he roared, "or I'll make mince meat out of you."

Seeing that Mike meant business, Burns and his army retreated.

"Quick!" Mike hissed. "Lock the door. We'll keep that riff-raff out for tonight at least."

Healey had no sooner complied when all hell broke loose. Edgings, stones and bricks came hurtling through the windows, showering broken glass over Ryan and Healey. Blinds were ripped off and doors shattered, but the sawmill gang, fearing what Ryan might do with that axe, made no attempt to re-enter the hotel. Instead, they threw things and jeered at the proprietor.

Mike, mad through and through, hitched up his horse and drove to Prospect, where he got Deputy Sheriff Neison and Constable Dicky-Dick Jones out of bed and rushed them to the scene.

Hinckley lay quiet as a grave. Only the broken windows and the litter of sticks and stones on the floor of the Empire House bespoke of what had taken place.

Neisen and Jones went to various boarding houses, rousted out of bed the men whom Ryan and Healey had identified, and brought them to the ballroom of the hotel.

Johnny O'Brien, whom they had found lying on his bed with his clothes on, caused another flurry when he jumped out of a window of the ballroom in an effort to escape, but Hinckley citizens grabbed him the moment his feet hit the ground and returned him to custody. The whole company was ordered to appear before Justice Bill Morris in Prospect the next day at two o'clock.

News of the riot spread, and the ballroom of the Arnold House in Prospect was crammed with interested but not always polite spectators.

When District Attorney Klock had the men rearrested on the charge of riot, one of the prisoners raised a wail of protest. "I'se been pulled twicet, d'ye see?" he complained. "It don't go, see, and I'll have a gran' joory trial first, see."

Alex Burns said, disgustedly, "Oh, what the hell!"

Josiah Perry, a prominent lawyer from Utica, had been engaged by the defendants. All he could accomplish was to establish an alibi for Johnny O'Brien, who, on the stand, swore, to the vast amusement of the spectators, that he had downed four pints of whiskey during the day and had been too drunk to go out, so he had gone to bed with his clothes on, only to be pulled out of a deep sleep by Neison and Jones.

Justice Morris held all men except O'Brien for the action of the grand jury, which found Burns and Albert Lawer guilty of the charge of riot. They were each fined fifty dollars or a term of imprisonment not to exceed one day for each dollar of the fine.

STALEMATE

Back in 1895, when Hinckley was a boom town, E. G. Hargrave's lumber company employed 300 men and kindred industries gave work to many more. The village held a floating population of assorted characters who came from nowhere and usually disappeared in the same direction. Something had to be done to keep the workers from spending their money and energy in the four hotels which stood shoulder to shoulder on the main street.

Hargrave had brought with him from Bay City, Michigan, several good baseball players. His brother, Frank, played shortstop like a professional, and the Adams brothers, Bill and Harry, were also expert infielders. With these players forming a nucleus, a team was formed which was capable of battling any aggregation in the foothills.

No Hinckley native played on the team. George Hughes and Louis O'Leary, two of the outfielders, hailed from Trenton and Boonville, respectively. No one seemed to know where Jack Collins, the first baseman, came from, but, sober or half-shot, he drove in most of the runs. Behind the bat crouched Joe Bushy, a stocky, red-headed French-Canadian known for his pugnacious attitude and his ability to upset opposing hitters with well-chosen remarks. The two pitchers alternated between that position and left field. Lane often started games against weaker opponents and was replaced by Maurice Leary when he faltered. Leary, who boasted a terrific fastball, was one of the best pitchers in the foothills.

Hinckley had a team, but it had no place to play its games. Ben Van Etten, a farmer across the West Canada Creek, offered his pasture, and all of Hinckley pitched in to get the field ready. Games were staged each Saturday afternoon against teams from Middleville, Newport and Utica, and Hinckley mowed down most of the opposition with ridiculous ease.

Trenton, five miles down the creek, had boasted a good ball club for years. These players scoffed at the "lumberjacks," and it took considerable persuasion to get them to cross bats with the Hinckley "barbarians," but on August 21 they ran into Leary & Co. Their pitcher, Charlie French, was knocked out of the box in the seventh inning. The final score read: Hinckley 15, Trenton 5. Trenton, jolted to the heels, demanded a return game.

The rivals met at Van Etten Park on September 11. Some new faces could be seen in the Trenton lineup, including Gilmore, a star pitcher from Whitesboro. The first inning practically decided the contest, for Trenton, through the aid of some inept fielding on the part of the home team, scored seven runs and went on to win the game 22 to 9.

Hinckley folks did not take the defeat in stride. They complained about the Trenton "ringers," intimated that the visitors had paid the umpire, and challenged their rivals to a rubber game for any sum between $25 and $100. The Trenton players ignored the challenge.

Hinckley stewed in its juice all winter, but came out in the spring wearing new uniforms raised by public subscription. It not only beat Boonville on the latter's home grounds but came out ahead in both games of a home-and-home series with Forestport, which boasted the Kernan brothers and other top-notch collegians.

Trenton was pressured into a game on August 7th, and all of Hinckley descended on that sedate village to see their heroes win the contest 21 to 17. The jubilant Hinckley reporter to the *Boonville Herald* used poetry to describe the victory.

Trenton came to Van Etten Park on September 12th with a do-or-die attitude. Gilmore again pitched and several Utica stars dotted the lineup, despite the protests of Hinckley. Trenton jumped on Leary for three runs in the first inning, but Hinckley came back with two in its half and tied the score with a run in the fourth. Trenton pushed across a tally in the seventh and the score stood 4 to 3 when Hinckley came to bat in the last of the ninth.

Leary opened that frame with a single and stole second. O'Leary hit a ball back at Gilmore, who knocked it down. Leary, thinking the Trenton pitcher had lost control of the ball, lit out for third, where he was tagged out. Lawler, the next batter, clouted the pill far into left field. O'Leary, sure that he could score from first with the tying run, was rounding third when he discovered that Patton, the Trenton left fielder, had made a circus catch of Lawler's drive and had doubled him up for the final out.

When Hinckley recovered from the shock, it challenged Trenton to a game to be played at Utica Park for $100, but Trenton rested on its laurels and snow spread a blanket over the season.

ROBINSON THE GREAT

Though Hinckley seldom lacked displays of fisticuffs, whether engaged in by small boys on the main street or by lumberjacks in one of the hotels, local pride deplored the fact that no real prize fight between professionals had ever been staged in the village.

In the fall of 1895, when Hinckley residents were still boasting about their baseball team, who should put in an appearance but a smooth-talking, stockily-built fellow who introduced himself as Joe Robinson the Great, the middleweight champion of Maine. Robinson admitted that he would take on any man of his weight for any purse up to fifty dollars a side.

Hinckley took Robinson to its collective bosom and a ten-round bout was soon arranged between the Maine champion and the middleweight king of northern New York, George Scribner. As prize fights did not meet with the approval of Oneida County officials, it was decided to hold the bout in Roberge's Grove in Grant, a place sufficiently isolated on the Herkimer County side of the West Canada Creek to cause authorities to wink an eye at proceedings held there. Tickets at one dollar a head went like hot cakes and Hinckley could talk of only one thing—the great prize fight.

Robinson the Great went into training behind Fred Morrison's hotel before countless admirers and boasted what he would do to the upstart who had accepted his challenge. He evidently talked so loudly that wind of the approaching contest blew as far as Tupper Lake, and Deputy Sheriff Neison of Prospect received orders to arrest the Maine champion for jumping a board bill in that Adirondack village. Hinckley sports rescued Joe by paying the money, and boxing fans from all the surrounding area assembled in Roberge's Grove on a Friday night to see the scrap. Unfortunately, Scribner failed to show up, so all the crowd got for a dollar a head was a series of preliminary bouts.

Undaunted, the sports, led by Fred Morrison of the Century Hotel, kept the wires hot and secured for Robinson's next opponent a pug by the name of Teddy McMahon, who enjoyed a reputation around Oneida. Joe promised to give McMahon a lively run for his money. McMahon arrived on the afternoon train, looking fit.

The promoters had planned to stage the bout in one of the barns behind the hotels, but Neison put a stop to the foolishness, so hasty arrangements were made to hold the affair behind a roadhouse Roselle Halliday operated about a mile up the creek toward Grant. Groups of men could be seen strolling across the bridge as dusk fell and, after Neison left for Prospect, horses and buggies dashed madly across the creek toward the Halliday House.

The ring had been staked out when they arrived, and Robinson and McMahon sat in their respective corners, coats thrown over their shoulders. Most of the money had been placed on Robinson, for little was known of McMahon.

Excitement rose as the two boxers threw off their coats and advanced to the center of the ring. They sparred for a few minutes and threw a punch or two. Suddenly, Robinson rushed McMahon and fell into a clinch. They wrestled around, each trying to throw the other.

McMahon let out a piercing cry of pain. He wrestled out of the clinch and put both hands to his chest. Blood trickled through his fingers and down his bare torso. And the crowd sensed that the great Robinson had deliberately bitten his opponent.

Robinson backed away and muttered, "I don't know why I did it. I must have lost my head." Then, sensing the hostility of the crowd, he grabbed his clothes and beat a hasty retreat toward Hinckley.

A terrific uproar went up from the baffled spectators. Some wanted to lynch Robinson, or at least give him a coat of tar and feathers; others were yelling for payment of their wagers.

The Halliday House wasn't far from the creek, which was packed solidly with logs for the sawmill at Hinckley. A man could be seen dancing across the logs. It turned out that he carried with him much of the money which was to go to the supporters of McMahon. Old timers say Fred Morrison had a hand in the matter, but no proof ever came to light.

Teddy McMahon took the affair in stride. Though badly bitten, he picked up his fifty bucks and was driven to Hinckley, where a doctor patched him up and put him on a train for Oneida. Teddy later fought out of Boonville and also played third base for the local baseball team.

Robinson the Great? He had vanished into the night.

WILD BILL AND THE WOODCHOPPERS

Forestport took baseball seriously in 1898. Games were played on the Dutch Hill diamond, and the five sawmills would close down so that the workers could cheer the local heroes. Each evening, the steps of O'Connor's Hotel would be lined with players, fans and small boys, discussing the pros and cons of each contest.

The season started on the Fourth of July. Forestport travelled to Boonville for a morning contest and held the lead until the last of the ninth inning, when the home team pushed across four runs to win the game 14-13. The Forestport players, after listening to several holiday orations, got revenge on Boonville at Dutch Hill by trouncing the visitors 23-1, thus insuring success to the evening's display of fireworks.

A team from Utica came to Forestport, bringing with them Wild Bill Setley, a former pitcher in the New York State League. Wild Bill had a gift for gab, and some folks claim that he talked himself out of professional ball. On this occasion, he played second base. When a ball took an erratic bounce over the shortstop's shoulder, Wild Bill incurred the hatred of all Forestport by remarking, "This land is so poor you can't raise an umbrella on it." During the exchange of pleasantries which followed, Wild Bill added insult to injury by referring to the Forestport players as "a bunch of woodchoppers."

Forestport folks had no objection to being called woodchoppers, for many of the men spent part of each year in the woods, but the players, with the exception of Frank Connors, the local grocer, were college stars who had been assembled by the sons of John D. Kernan, a Utica lawyer who summered with his family in Forestport.

Four Kernan sons played. Frank, a hot-headed young fellow, hit the longest ball; Bob, who alternated between the outfield and second base, was the best all-around player; Devereux and Hubert, mere youngsters, filled in where needed. Five Cornell stars camped for the summer near the state dam. Heatley Green, a top-flight catcher, led the team in batting; the Costellos, Toots and Frank, were expert infielders, and the latter, though left-handed, covered second base when he was not pitching. Two Dissels came, one playing first base and the other throwing his fast ball when Hank Costello wasn't on the mound.

To complete the array of talent, Tickle Williams of Williams College showed the foothills how third base should be played.

Forestport's chief rivals were Boonville and Hinckley, the latter a team which had humiliated them a few years before, but which had lost many of its star players. Great was the joy in Forestport when the local heroes trounced their rivals from the West Canada Creek 15-2. Hinckley immediately demanded and got a second chance.

When Forestport's players arrived at Van Etten Park, who should stride out to the mound for Hinckley but Wild Bill Setley? The lanky hurler had a good day. He threw his fastball past the Forestport hitters and Hinckley won the game 7-4. Wild Bill kept the necks of the collegians red by passing remarks about the "woodchoppers." To top everything, he told the Utica papers that he had made two doubles and two singles and had struck out a dozen Forestport batters. A check of the Forestport scorebook showed that the great man had made no hits and had fanned four.

He had succeeded in fanning the dispositions of the Forestport players, who were still seething when they journeyed to Trenton Falls to play a team they had beaten earlier in the season 16-3. Wild Bill was again on hand, this time to pitch for Trenton Falls. He sauntered casually over to the Forestport bench before the game and asked, "How do you woodchoppers hope to win a game when I'm pitching against you?"

Forestport almost made the great man swallow his words. They tagged him for twelve hits and seven runs, but some inept fielding gave Trenton Falls eight tallies and the victory. Wild Bill, shaken to the heels by this close shave, had no comeback when a Forestport player remarked, "Wild Bill may do for the State League, but he is too slow for the woodchoppers."

The rubber game with Hinckley was scheduled for the next Saturday, so the real choppers turned out in droves at Dutch Hill to give the loud-mouthed pitcher a hard time. Hinckley brought along a few ringers, but Wild Bill had chosen to stay in Utica. Evidently he had gained respect for the "woodchoppers."

Forestport beat Hinckley, also Port Leyden and some Utica teams, but the crowning achievement came at the Boonville Fair, when Hank Costello, breaking off his slow curve better than ever before, beat the Boonville team 4-3 in ten innings.

FIRE IN THE NIGHT

A woman on the outskirts of Forestport woke up at two-thirty on the morning of February 9, 1899. She looked out the window and saw a glow in the sky. Inasmuch as the Spanish-American War was in progress, she woke her family and cried, "Get up, all of you. The war is coming this way!"

The boys climbed into their clothes in a jiffy, but the father, true to form, lit his corncob pipe and made for the backhouse to ponder the situation.

When the boys reached the village, it seemed as if all hell had broken loose. The Getman House was afire, and men were racing in and out, carrying out Dick Manahan's stock. Dick, sensing that the building would go, said, "Never mind me, boys. Take what you want for yourselves." Several potential fire-fighters got sidetracked by the more interesting task of carrying bottles from the burning hotel.

The Forestport fire-fighters were short-handed, for many able-bodied men were lumbering in the woods, but the old hand-pumper was dragged to the Black River and hose was strung to the burning hotel. The thermometer registered below zero, and the ice had to be cracked to put the end of the hose into the stream. The first energetic work on the brakes sent chunks of ice into the hose and blocked passage of the water. The Getman House was a mass of flames before the firemen got a stream on it. John Neegar, the village butcher, hitched up his horses and drove madly toward Boonville for help.

The fire swept northward along River Street, taking with it Forestport's other three hotels, its saloon, its undertaking establishment, Helmer's store and several houses and barns.

The boys ran from building to building, helping to take out a stove here, a dresser there. When the O'Connor Hotel caught fire, a commode containing a half-filled chamber mug was carried from the upper floor. One man, in his excitement, picked up the mug and carried it up and down the stairs several times before the boys' laughter caused him to hurl the mug angrily to the street, where it shattered—and spattered.

In the meanwhile, the church women were busy brewing coffee for the fire-fighters, so one of our boys was delegated to carry pitchers of the steaming liquid down the street. He encountered a fellow who had accepted Manahan's invitation and was carrying a quantity of Dick's fluid inside him and was waving a bottle in each hand.

"What you got there, boy?" he asked.

"Coffee."

"I'll warm it up for you," said the drunk, emptying the contents of the bottles into the pitchers.

The boy said nothing, but went about delivering his goods. Temperance folks remarked that they had never tasted better coffee and had several cups each.

All of Forestport was either fighting fire, removing furniture, or acting as spectators. One woman holding a rather precocious child in her arms could not stop him from singing at the top of his lungs the popular song of the day, "It's a Hot Time in the Old Town Tonight."

The final desperate stand by the fire-fighters was made at John Helmer's house, which stood close to the burning O'Connor Hotel. Henry Utley and Jim Rudolph carried the hose to the piazza roof of the Helmer house and played water on the building. Ed Marshall hazarded his life by shinnying to the upper balcony of the burning hotel and tying a rope to a post so that the balcony could be pulled away from the Helmer house. The spectators rewarded Ed with a round of applause when he came down, just as the Boonville department arrived after a record run.

Dawn showed a scene of desolation. Fourteen buildings had been burned. The eastern side of River Street had been swept clean. The only thing still active was Dick Manahan's liquor. Two drunks wrestled in the street. One got the other down and tried to pummel him, but each time he would aim a punch, the underdog would turn his head with the result that the victor nearly broke his hands hitting the pavement.

He was one of few casualties. One man sprained an ankle and there was a collection of frozen ears, noses and toes. And, sad to relate, some of the Forestport church folks, including the superintendent of the Sunday school, carried hangovers from drinking coffee too early in the morning.

LITTLE ITALY

The construction of the state dam at Hinckley wiped out two picturesque settlements which straggled toward Northwood and Grant on opposite sides of the West Canada Creek. Little Brooklyn, on the Herkimer County bank, was populated chiefly by Polish immigrants, while Little Italy, as its name implies, swarmed with refugees from the sunny Mediterranean who had been employed in building the spur line of the Adirondack & St. Lawrence Railroad from Prospect Junction to Hinckley.

As might be expected, Little Italy was by far the more colorful settlement. Families were large, and it took a pretty skillful driver to navigate his horse and buggy through the dusty street without killing or maiming a child, a dog or a hen.

Little Italy was not noted for its cleanliness, so the Consolidated Water Company, which supplied Utica with water from a point further up the creek, employed a patrolman who went around picking up refuse and enjoining the inhabitants to throw less garbage into the street.

The patrolman, Dick Briggs, was making his rounds one Saturday when he tangled with a woman with the picturesque name of Mrs. Dominaco Zincorello. Briggs was trying to get her to clean up her back yard so he could cart away some of the refuse. After considerable "chin play" from Mrs. Zincorello, Briggs was able to collect three baskets of garbage, tin cans, etc., and take them to his cart.

The argument continued when Briggs returned for a fourth basketful, and in the course of the affair, Mrs. Zincorello tore a picket from her fence and lambasted the patrolman with it until his arm was black and blue, while she perfumed the air with words of many odors.

Briggs had taken plenty of abuse from the inhabitants of Little Italy, so he had the lady arrested. The trial before Justice John O. Pritchard of Remsen brought more fireworks. Mrs. Zincorello contended that Briggs had flirted with her and that she had used the picket to defend her honor. This line of argument amused the room full of spectators more than it did the justice, who fined her fifteen dollars or fifteen days in jail, then suspended sentence during good behavior.

Two years later, Tony Masch held a christening of a baby which had blessed his home. Tony, happy about the event, had invited most of Little Italy and had provided plenty of "wet goods" to keep his guests in good humor. The day was Sunday, and Little Italy rang with the sound of the accordion, singing and dancing all afternoon.

Jim Mocculdi and his wife and daughter had paid their respects to the keg on numerous occasions, so by six o'clock they were the happiest family in Little Italy. When the second keg was tapped, the Mocculdis were first in line. Here they encountered Tony Quaito, with whom they had been at odds for some time. The old argument was resumed in front of the keg and of all Little Italy. Quaito, overwhelmed by numbers, escaped from the two women, who were pelting him merrily, and ran into the yard, only to find Mocculdi waiting for him at the gate. Ripping off pickets was evidently a custom in Little Italy, for when the harassed Quaito tried to scale the fence, Jim grabbed a picket and belted him with it. He was putting on a few artistic touches with his knife when Joe and Tony Monaco took sides with Quaito and attacked Mocculdi, starting a free for all which spoiled the christening party.

Little Italy awoke at dawn and rigs filled with Italians raised dust as they raced down the road toward Prospect. Their destination was Remsen, the home of the harassed Justice Pritchard. Mocculdi, having secured the speediest team from the Hinckley livery, reached Remsen first, got the Justice out of bed, and had warrants sworn out for the arrest of Joe Monaco and Anthony Quaito.

Hinckley folks usually let Little Italy go its way, but a serious case caused them to rise up against the offender. Joe Jerman looked, acted and was bad. He came to Hinckley to work in the lumbermill. Later, he brought his eighteen-year-old daughter, Louisa, to keep house for him and his two sons. Louisa did not please her father, who threatened to do away with her. Louisa, badly frightened, took refuge with neighbors. Joe didn't like this turn in affairs, so he went to her boarding place, flourished a knife and cried that he would kill her. Friends had Louisa swear out a warrant, and Deputy Sheriff Neison arrested Jerman. No one in Little Italy would go bond for him, so he was packed off to jail, while Hinckley breathed a collective sigh of relief.

UNCLE TOM'S CABIN

No village in the Adirondack foothills a half century ago could endure a year without at least one performance of "Uncle Tom's Cabin." The Comstock Opera House in Boonville made it standard repertory, while tent shows wandered from village to village each summer, supplying the needs of the people for "stirring drama."

One evening in 1901, the Shipman troupe was performing in Prospect, and the large audience was commenting on how much Simon Legree looked like John Shiner, the lumberman, when a thunderstorm struck and lifted the tent from its moorings. Panic ensued as Prospect citizens disentangled themselves from canvas and ropes and rushed here and there, trying to collect their numerous offspring. Fortunately, no one was injured, though everyone got drenched to the skin. The Shipman folks, being good troupers, told the Prospectors to go home and put on dry clothes. Later in the evening, they staged a vaudeville show at the Walters Opera House—which was merely a hall with a high-sounding name—and entertained the home folks well into the night.

When Downing McPhee and his company appeared in Forestport the next summer and began to erect tents, the usual crowd of children milled around the grounds while committees of oldsters lent unsolicited advice to the workmen.

Rob Putney drove up with Frank Connors' brown mare and delivery wagon to take a peek at proceedings before finishing his deliveries. He drove a little too close to the rising tent and the mare, in trying to clear the guy ropes, jumped a bit too high. The bolt holding the whiffle-tree broke and let the thills drop. Rob got jolted from the seat and landed on his chin in front of the wagon. The mare, badly frightened, fought clear and dashed off, carrying the whiffle-tree and part of the harness with her. Each time she would slow down, the whiffle-tree would bang her on the heels. Completely losing sense of direction, she barged into Bill Shanks' wire fence, rolled over several times, freed herself and dashed madly up the White Lake road. T. M. Wenner jumped into his grain wagon and drove after her. A second wire fence, this one belonging to Jerome Potter, proved to be an obstacle she could not surmount, so Wenner untangled her and led her to Forestport.

"Uncle Tom's Cabin" usually brought along an assortment of followers, who had no connection with the troupes but liked to tag along for excitement. McPhee's company was no exception. One fellow who had loaded up at the Forestport bars began the afternoon auspiciously by going to F. X. Salzman's barn, where he tied a rope around a calf's neck and tried to lead it off. Salzman, arriving in the nick of time, was able to persuade the drunk to leave the calf behind.

The fellow shifted his talents to stone-throwing. He staggered up the road leading to the show grounds, abusing Forestport people and hurling stones at any conceivable object. When he reached the house of James Fuller, he decided he would go in and pay a call. Mrs. Fuller did not take kindly to this intrusion. When she would not let him in, he not only abused her, but bounced an umbrella over the head of eighty-year-old Gould Denslow, who attempted to be her knight-errant. He ended up by slamming the gate on Mrs. Fuller, pinning her in and hurting her.

About this time, McPhee and Wenner, having captured Connors' mare, heard the commotion and came on the run. The intruder pretended to draw a gun, but McPhee ignored this gesture, took him by the scruff of the neck and gave him a good thrashing. The fellow staggered back toward Forestport, badly the worse for wear, while McPhee went back to the business of preparing the tent for the evening's performance.

Justice moved at a snail's pace in Forestport, so it was late afternoon before Constable Nightengale arrested the man and took him to the Manahan Hotel.

As dusk broke over Forestport, and most of the folks were climbing the hill toward the show grounds, the center of the village rang with excitement. Nightengale's prisoner, somewhat sobered up after his beating and arrest, dashed out of the hotel and headed toward the bridge over the Black River. The constable and others, crying "stop thief," lit out after him. The prisoner, spurred on by the fear of further punishment and possible imprisonment, raced across the bridge like an Olympic quarter-miler and was swallowed up in the gloom beyond the river.

"Uncle Tom's Cabin?" Despite the hectic events of the day, it is said that the audience thoroughly enjoyed the show.

IV. FOLKS

I write of foothills folks of yesterday
Who carved no niche in any hall of fame,
But, in their simple manner, played the game
Of life, each in his own peculiar way.
For some the road was sad, for others gay,
But each tale in its unimportant frame
May add a touch of lustre to a name
Before the passing years wash it away.

A country doctor, gruff as man could be;
A redhead that a village could not tame;
A preacher fighting for woman's name;
A long-haired orator who crossed the sea;
At them and Allie, chuckle, as you may,
But shed a gentle tear for May Ann Day.

THE SEARCH

In the years before the Civil War, nearly everyone from Utica to Watertown was familiar with the story of May Ann Day, the mild, inoffensive woman who wandered from farm to farm, fair weather or foul, in her search for two people who had dropped out of her life years before.

May's parents had died when she was a teen-aged girl, leaving her and a sister several years younger. May idealized her sister, who was intelligent and attractive. May worked her hands to the bone, earning money so that she could send the younger girl to a private school in Utica, and looked forward to the day when the apple of her eye would marry a fine, upstanding man.

The sister fell in love and became engaged. The young man postponed the wedding until he could be in a better position to support her, and May spent her days and nights earning money to provide a church wedding for her sister. At last the day was set. May bought expensive wedding clothes for her sister and thrilled at the thought of seeing her married in style.

She patched her best dress and put a few new ornaments on her bonnet. She walked on air as she made her way to the church. All of her drudgery seemed worthwhile. Her sister would be married in church, wearing the best dress money could buy. She reached the door to find the minister waiting alone. Neither the bride nor the groom had put in an appearance. They had eloped!

The significance of their act did not impress itself on May's mind right away. She waited and waited, until the minister told her kindly that he did not think the couple would appear. May went back to her humble room, removed the hat with its new trimmings, fell down on the bed and wept bitterly.

It was her last rational act, for from that day her mind grew hopelessly confused. She imagined that the groom was her lover and that he had jilted her in order to run away with her sister. She took to the road, continually walking from village to village, trying to recognize two faces which people felt that she was never destined to see, for the young people had no intention of informing her of their whereabouts.

May was a pretty woman, immaculate in her person and clean in her habits. She would appear at a farmhouse, ask gently for work, and become part of the household. She was a good worker, and housewives welcomed her help. No one ever got to know her, for she seldom spoke, except to answer questions in a soft, cultured voice. She seldom stayed more than a few days. A restlessness would overcome her, and she would talk to herself in an incoherent flood of words from which the people picked out her sad story. Folks would usually wake up in the morning to find her gone. She would be tramping the roads again, scanning the faces of people she met and shaking her head sadly.

May Ann Day wandered through the Adirondack foothills for over thirty years, until she became a legend to the farmers and villagers. As her footsteps became heavier, her mind cracked completely, so that she became a hopeless lunatic. The authorities felt that she could no longer take care of herself, so they committed her to the County House in Rome.

May did not relinquish her search, though she no longer wandered along the roads. She examined carefully the face of each man and woman who was brought to the County House. At last she grew so old and feeble that she could hardly get around. It seemed that her life-long quest had been in vain.

One day the feeble wreck of a man was carried into the building. His face was lined with pain and his body wasted by years of dissipation. May got a good luck at him and recognized him as the man who had eloped with her sister many years before. She uttered one terrifying shriek, and dropped dead.

May Ann Day's search was over, but her story remained on the tongues of the people for many a year.

THE LONG-HAIRED ORATOR

The Lyon family was well established in Lyonsdale when a boy was born on December 7, 1822 and named Caleb, according to a family custom of naming the youngest son after the father. Franklin B. Hough, in his *History of Lewis County,* states that young Caleb got his early training from Rev. John Sherman of Trenton. If so, the youngster must have been precocious, for Mr. Sherman died in 1828, when Caleb was six years of age. Caleb graduated from Lowville Academy and from Norwich University in Northfield, Vermont, before going on to Montreal for advanced study. When he returned to Lyonsdale, he probably was the best-educated man in the Adirondack foothills.

Like many talented youths of his day, Caleb wrote poetry, including one epic concerning Father Pierre Joulin, a Jesuit who came to the Black River country with the emigres. He also cultivated an eccentricity in dress. He let his hair grow to his shoulders, and sported a mustache and a VanDyke beard at a time when most men went smooth-shaven.

Caleb Lyon was about twenty-five years of age when he shook the dust of Lyonsdale from his heels and migrated to the nation's capital, where President James K. Polk and members of Congress became impressed with his ability. In 1847, Caleb's name was brought before the United States Senate as a nominee for the post of consul to Shanghai. Some of the senators raised objections to his appearance. Colonel Thomas Hart Benton of Missouri said he "would not be guilty of voting to send a man with such hair and beard out of the country."

Lyon was brought before Benton's committee and listened calmly to the senatorial objections. At the close, he rose and said, "Make my compliments to those grave and revered senators; thank them for the great honor they paid me and say to them if I go as consul to Shanghai, I go as God made me, or not at all." Benton, favorably impressed by the young man's sincerity, got Lyon the appointment.

Here Caleb did one of the many flip-flops which were to characterize his career. He chose not to go to Shanghai, but sent a deputy to represent him. The gold rush in California had attracted his fancy, so off he went to the West Coast. In this wild and uncultured atmosphere, the man from Lyonsdale evidently made a hit with his appearance and his oratory. He was chosen one of the secretaries of the constitutional convention. When a $1,000 prize was offered for the best design for the state seal of California, Caleb turned out the drawing which won the prize.

He soon tired of California and came back to Lyonsdale, where he was elected to the state assembly as an independent in 1850. The following year, he ran for the state senate and encountered considerable opposition. "They not only send against me their war-horses clothed in thunder," he cried, "but their asses laden with silver." He won the election.

Distant fields always seemed greener to Caleb Lyon, so in 1852 he ran for Congress, where he served one term and was defeated for re-election. Undaunted, he dashed off on a tour of Europe and the Near East. He was probably the first man from the foothills to see Turkey, Egypt and Palestine. He returned to Lyonsdale, built a fine house, and filled it with treasures he had picked up on his travels.

Norwich University had presented him with the degree of L.L.D. in 1851. Caleb continued his scholarly pursuits by bringing a fine collection of manuscripts and autographed letters to Lyonsdale.

His brother, Lyman, who was about sixteen years his senior, evidently did not approve of Caleb's way of life. The disagreements came to a head when a minister named Bacon was accused of slitting his wife's throat in Lyonsdale. It is said that Lyon took a horsewhip to Caleb, right on the main street of the village.

Caleb, nonplussed, went on with his career. He was the favorite orator at patriotic celebrations except for a short time during the Civil War, when President Lincoln appointed him territorial governor of Idaho.

An old account tells how Caleb spoke in Willard's woods in Boonville one Fourth of July. He made such a favorable impression that, later, he was called to the balcony of Hulbert's Hotel. To cries of "Lyon! Lyon! Lyon!" the long-haired orator bowed and delivered an impromptu speech.

The foothills lost Caleb Lyon when his home in Lyonsdale, with its collection of treasures, went up in smoke. He moved to Staten Island, where he finished out his years.

OLD MORRIS

Old Morris is coming! The cry would rise from the children playing in the yard. It would carry to their mother, who would hurry to prepare a cup of tea and a few cakes. The father also would hear the cry, and would come in from the barn to tidy up a bit for his guest. The children, awe-stricken by the approach of the mighty preacher, would watch from behind bushes near the house.

Old Morris moved slowly, for he was approaching his eightieth year. His massive shoulders had succumbed to a slight stoop and a heaviness had crept into his sturdy legs, but his smooth-shaven face, ruddy beneath the thatch of white hair, held scarcely a wrinkle and his sharp eyes had lost little of their glitter.

The children would watch while the aged preacher entered the house, had tea with their parents, and walked toward the road again.

Rev. Morris Roberts, even during his lifetime, became a legend in Remsen. He had come to the village from Wales in 1833 to preach at the Stone Church. His oratory had met with such an enthusiastic response that the Calvinistic Methodists elected him to succeed Rev. David Stephens, a pastor who had worked himself to the bone to raise money for the church, and whose rejection resulted in his death of heart-break.

Old Morris, in his youth, was said to have been a "veritable son of Thunder." His resonant voice boomed forth in denunciation of evil, yet he could control it so that his words would carry when he lowered his tones to a whisper. And his commanding stature and piercing eyes added emphasis to his words.

Dr. Roberts' thinking was far ahead of his times. He denounced slavery and alcoholism and attacked the hide-bound ideas of his own church. When he preached a sermon on the power of man, his theories were considered so unorthodox that he was asked to recant by the ruling body of elders. He not only refused, but preached more sermons on the subject. The congregation took sides. The elders brought Rev. William Rowlands up from Utica to debate the matter with Mr. Roberts. The debates brought about a split in the church. Mr. Roberts withdrew and took half of the congregation with him.

Mr. Roberts was not beaten—nor half-beaten. He set sail on a tour of Western New York and Eastern Ohio, collecting funds to build a new church in Remsen under the Congregational form of government. About 1841, he and his followers erected Peniel Church, where he thundered forth his denunciations of evil for forty years. He also was instrumental in rebuilding Bethel chapel four miles above Remsen.

Late in life, Old Morris ran into difficulty with his parishioners over another matter. There were living, on the outskirts of Remsen, an unmarried woman with her ten-year-old son. Old Morris decided that the mother should be admitted to Peniel Church, so that the boy could be brought up in a religious atmosphere. The ruling body, usually docile, refused to accept the woman, despite Old Morris' pleading.

The aged preacher, not accustomed to rebuffs, defied the church fathers. Each communion Sunday, accompanied by the one elder who had stuck with him, Old Morris walked down the dusty road to the woman's house, where he spread the cloth for Ellen and her little boy, and took communion with them. The members of the church, though they were aware of their minister's breach of etiquette, refused to acknowledge it; nor would they stir one inch toward accepting Ellen into their church body.

One June Sunday in 1878, people on their way to the Remsen churches noted an extreme stillness in the village. The leaves hung limply from the trees. Even the song birds chose to be silent. From person to person passed the whispered question, "Did you hear?" and the answer, "Old Morris is dead!"

The familiar white-haired figure no longer would appear at their doors; the voice which had denounced narrow-mindedness, slavery and alcoholism had been silenced forever.

Peniel Church was filled to overflowing for the funeral and a long cortege followed Old Morris to the graveyard.

Outside the cemetery wall, dressed in black, stood a frail woman, holding by the hand a ten-year-old boy. Ellen was weeping bitterly, for she had lost her only friend.

A PRESIDENT COMES HOME

Holland Patent assumed a festive mood, for President Grover Cleveland was to bring his new wife to The Weeds, the Cleveland family home. Plans had been formulated to meet the couple when their special train pulled in at noon. The Cleveland house had been made ready by Miss Rose Elizabeth to accommodate the expected guests.

Grover had always baffled Holland Patent. To the local people, the burly politician seemed more at home playing cards with Dr. D. A. Crane or fishing for trout in a nearby brook than he did in the office of President of the United States. Most of the voters in this Republican stronghold looked askance at a Democrat, though many of them had voted for their favorite son in the last election.

The morning train rolled into Holland Patent between eight and nine with a special car attached. Grover Cleveland and his bride got off, checked their trunks and started out on foot for The Weeds. They had caught the villagers napping.

Once in his family home, the President put on a straw hat and a linen duster and went browsing in the garden, which was surrounded by a fence.

"Hello, Grove, that you?"

Cleveland looked up to see his friend, Dr. Crane, sitting erect in his gig and peering over the fence at him.

"Doing anything important?" asked the doctor. "I'm going up the road a mile or two to see a sick woman. Would you like to ride along?"

Cleveland changed his hat and coat, got into the gig beside the doctor, who clicked to the horse. The gig rolled up the street.

"How's everything in Washington, Grove?"

"Fine, Doc, and I want to tell you I'd never got there if it hadn't been for your vote."

Dr. Crane chuckled. "You know, Grove, after voting Republican for years, I wanted to vote for a man I knew, instead of voting for men I never saw or met."

The President held the reins while Dr. Crane went into a farmhouse to see his patient.

The woman's husband, a hard-headed farmer of Welsh extraction, came to the road. "Come up from the Patent?" he asked by way of starting a conversation.

"Yes."

"Friend of Doc Crane?"

"Yes."

"Going to have great times down in the Patent this afternoon, I hear. Rose Elizabeth, she's going to give a reception to her brother and his wife. Nearly everybody is going."

"Are you going?"

"No, I ain't. I didn't vote for him, and while I've nothing agin him, I don't think he's any man to be President. Least ways, you know I voted for the other man, and a man naturally wants his party to succeed."

"That's so, and I quite agree with you about the man who was elected. Fishing, it seems to me, would suit him better."

"There you're right," rejoined the farmer. "You know him?"

"I've met him, and I think I know him pretty well."

Dr. Crane came out and said to the farmer, "I see you have been talking with my friend."

"Yes, seeing he was your friend, I thought I would talk to him."

"Don't you know him?"

"Never saw him in my life that I remember."

"Well, this is President Cleveland, and I am glad to introduce you to him."

The farmer turned on the doctor. "If that's President Cleveland, I'd like to know what a Republican like you is doing riding with him."

The President and the village doctor drove off, enjoying a hearty laugh when out of earshot of the farmer.

The farmer's little girl stood beside the road. "Doctor," she asked, "are you going to the reception at the Patent this afternoon?"

"I guess so. Are you going?"

"I don't think I can, but I'd like to, because I want to see Mrs. Cleveland. I think she is the most beautiful woman in the world."

"You come," said Mr. Cleveland. "I'll introduce you to her."

The little girl attended the reception and remembered all her life how Mrs. Cleveland took her in her arms and kissed her.

She went home and told her father, who said, "Glad you enjoyed yourself. But I can't get over Dr. Crane riding with a Democrat."

BOONVILLE GETS A FAIR

Boonville has always possessed a generous measure of civic pride. It became the terminal of the first railroad to climb into the Adirondack foothills. It organized the famous Conkling Rifles and drilled that regiment in its fields. It was sending Charlie Phelps' buckboards over the Brown Tract Road to Arnold's on the Fulton Chain.

In one respect, however, the village was falling sadly behind. In 1888, when Lowville was advertising its 67th fair, Rome its 48th and little Trenton its 28th, the old Boonville Union Agricultural Society, which had carried on haphazardly for years found its buildings in dilapidated ruins.

Something had to be done to save face, so a group of prominent Boonville citizens got their heads and purses together in June and founded the Boonville Fair Association. They elected officers as follows: president, Milton J. Hoyt; vice-president, Charles T. Thompson; secretary, Frank W. Owen; treasurer, Robert H. Roberts. The association engaged W. H. Cole of Leyden as general superintendent and announced that they would put on the best fair Boonville had ever seen on September 11, 12, 13 and 14.

The summer was filled with feverish activity. The association leased the Driving Park, bounded by Summit, Schuyler and Ford Streets, for ten years. Exhibition buildings went up as if by magic. Horse sheds 300 feet long and cattle sheds 500 feet in length spread rapidly over the grounds and, to top everything, a "monster" grandstand, which seated over 1,200 people and had underneath it a dining room and a secretary's office, completed the building program.

Much of this activity was carried on under a shadow of sorrow, for the treasurer, "Bob" Roberts, a Welshman much beloved by the people of Boonville, had been killed instantly during the summer when a canal boat he had been constructing fell on him while he and his men were attempting to raise it.

Public support had been solicited, and by the time the fair opened on September 11, 100 season tickets had been sold. The fair got under way under bright, sunny skies. The exhibition buildings resplendent in red and green paint and decorated with flags and bunting, brought exclamations of delight from the 3,000 people who watched the stirring contest between three village bands. Port Leyden took the first prize of $40, with the Boonville Brass Band second and the Forestport Temperance Cornet Band third. Much time was spent by spectators viewing the exhibition halls, where displays of women's fancy work drew the largest crowds. And, for the farmers, B. O. Jackson exhibited a hog weighing 801 pounds.

Horse racing featured the second day's program. The contests were one-sided, for Charles Kilkenny of Boonville won all three heats in the race for four-year-olds with his Prince Albert, while H. Smith's Gold Diamond ran off with all three in the two-forty class.

The Boonville Fair got its first taste of the rain which would plague it for years on Thursday afternoon, but "Prof." Charles E. Slocum of Prospect made a balloon ascension at 4:30 and landed on the farm of George Farley near Forestport.

The main event of the fair was to take place on the fourth and final day, when Mrs. Belva Lockwood, a famous advocate of rights for women, was to make an address. Boonville showed Mrs. Lockwood a real reception. When her train pulled into the village about nine o'clock on Thursday night, over 1,000 people had gathered at the depot. The three brass bands marched, and a sea of lighted torches followed them as they escorted the village's guest to the home of Mrs. Frances Schultz on Schuyler Street.

Mrs. Lockwood visited the fair grounds the following morning, chiefly to see the horses. George W. Greene of Forestport brought out a dark gray two-year-old mare and asked Mrs. Lockwood to name her. The lady took the mare's head in her hands and christened her Belva.

Seven thousand people heard her address in the afternoon. She was introduced by F. A. Willard of the *Boonville Herald*. Some of the women were shocked because this candidate for President on the Equal Rights ticket wore neither corset nor bustle, but all were enthralled by her dark eyes and silvery voice.

Yes, the first Boonville Fair was a tremendous success. Everyone had a good time, the association finished with money to spend on new buildings, and the pride of the village had been upheld.

"FURRINERS"

Laborers on the construction of the Adirondack & St. Lawrence Railroad consisted chiefly of European immigrants. Italians predominated in the foothills section from Poland to White Lake Corners, now Woodgate. Three camps thrived between Poland and Trenton Falls, a large settlement outside the former village, and smaller ones near the Plumb place and at Gravesville. Crews building the Hinckley spur camped at Prospect junction and along the Prospect-Hinckley plank road near the Pittman toll-gate. Remsen had a quota of over 200 living in boarding houses in the village.

Railroads and "furriners" became the chief topics of conversation for foothills villagers after the first trainload of Italians arrived in Poland in April, 1891. Older citizens of that village remember the bakery the Italians set up and the wonderful loaves it produced. They also recall how tough contractor Brady was with his help; they say he would knock a man over the head at the slightest provocation. The Poland end saw several accidents. An Italian was killed by a falling tree, an Irishman died after having both legs amputated by a rolling car, and William Hardie, a mason, fell forty feet from the new trestle at Trenton Falls onto the rocks below and lived to tell of his experience. One June day, several Italians were buried in a landslide but, according to a Poland reporter, "When exhumed six hours afterward, they appeared fresh as crickets, only a little dazzled by being brought to light so suddenly."

Prospect liked her "furriners." Old timers recall how gangs came up from the junction to shop at the stores, leaving in their wake a cloud of dust which almost obscured the village. And the people enjoyed a hearty laugh at a group of Italians who wandered through the fields, picking dandelions and singing grand opera. Unfortunately, one of the tenors caught his foot in a bear trap and had to have it extricated by an amused farmer. On another occasion, while two ladies were driving near the Pittman toll-gate, their horse became frightened by the noisy campers and bolted, upsetting the ladies into the road. This affair led to moving the camp to a spot away from the road, where the Italians could sing arias without disturbing travellers.

While the men were grading the Owens cut below the village, an Italian was braking on a car of dirt when the car behind him broke loose and born down upon him. Bill Sullivan, the boss, yelled for him to jump for his life, but the "furriner" did not understand English, so he set the brakes harder and was crushed to death between the two cars.

Remsen also lost one Italian, who was buried by fallen earth, but this village found more excitement on Christmas night, when a series of revolver shots aroused the populace. One Michael Cafaldo had entered the boarding home of Leonard Battista on Maple Avenue and had fired three shots in the darkness at a bed in which lay the Spina brothers, Rosario and Joseph. It turned out that Cafaldo had a grudge against Joseph, but his bullets had hit Rosario, who was taken to St. Elizabeth's Hospital in Utica. Remsen was shocked to learn that when Battista and his wife visited Rosario in the hospital, the lady threw both arms around the neck of the wounded man and smacked him on the lips, right in front of her husband.

Forestport also got into the act, for a wild man broke loose up at Purgatory and scared the daylights out of the Italians who worked there. He was an Englishman who evidently had been brooding over some secret crime of the past, for he kept yelling, "They are after me. I made the bullets but I didn't shoot her." He was captured and taken to the Utica State Hospital.

The following spring, when the railroad was almost completed to White Lake Corners, Battista's boarding house in Remsen caught fire. Remsen had no fire-fighting equipment, but citizens formed a bucket-brigade from the Cincinnati Creek to the burning building, while others stripped the Welsh Baptist Church of pulpit, pews, windows, lamps and carpets. The church caught fire and was destroyed, along with the boarding house.

A passenger on the first train to pass over the Adirondack & St. Lawrence had this to say about "furriners" living in shacks above Forestport: "At each of these camps one sees groups of laborers, the colored brother with a general looseness in his apparel and an openness of countenance; the picturesque Polander, with hair lighter than the color of his skin; the swarthy Italian, with very little of his dark face exposed from the folds of a red bandanna, in which the remainder of his head is swathed."

Folks sighed with relief when these "furriners" left for good.

THE UBIQUITOUS REDHEAD

The catcher for the Hinckley baseball team was a redheaded French-Canadian named Joe Bushy. On and off the field, Joe strutted around and boasted of his prowess with his fists. If any trouble was brewing, he was sure to be in the midst of it. Hinckley folks, who had seen him in action, had a hearty respect for his fists, so Joe played the part of bully to the hilt.

He strutted into George Shufelt's livery stable one afternoon and demanded the loan of a horse and buggy. Shufelt, who weighed about 120 pounds, told Bushy he owed too much in back bills and refused to let him take a horse, whereupon Joe sailed into the smaller man and was beating him merrily when who should walk in but Len Jones, the hardware merchant, also a little man who wore thick-lensed glasses. Len couldn't "lick a fly."

"You scoundrel," cried Jones. "You ought to be arrested."

Bushy made for Jones, who scurried out as fast as his legs would carry him.

"Run, damn you," Bushy cried after him, "but I'll have it out with you if it takes a year."

Jones attended services regularly at the Methodist Church across the West Canada Creek. He also was proud of the membership button from the Knights of Pythias, which he wore in his buttonhole. One Sunday, as Len was returning from church with an equally timid companion, Bushy jumped out from behind a pile of lumber and grabbed him.

Jones pointed to his button and said, "I suppose I could have you arrested for this."

"To hell with your button," jeered Bushy, punching Jones in the face and knocking off his glasses. A solid right knocked Jones down, whereupon Bushy kicked him merrily, all the while telling the hardware merchant what he thought of people who butted into other folks' business.

Len's companion had fled at the first hint of a scuffle, so the hardware merchant, stunned but not critically injured, dragged his battered carcass to Dr. Leander Swartwout of Prospect for necessary repairs.

Jones had meant business when he had mentioned apprehending Bushy, so he swore out a warrant for the redhead's arrest, and Constable Dicky-Dick Jones, who wore a badge the size of a tomato can, went to Hinckley and took Bushy in.

The trial was held before Justice Bill Morris in the Union Hotel at Prospect on the following day. Bushy was judged guilty of assault and battery and held in bail for appearance before the grand jury. While the amount of bail was being determined, Bushy chattered in his native tongue with a menacing group of French-Canadians who had come down from Hinckley to see that their hero received justice at the hands of Squire Morris.

Constable Jones, though conversant with Welsh, had no knowledge of French-Canadian and he didn't want things said about him that he did not understand, so he walked over to the group and told them to shut up.

Bushy took advantage of the confusion to dash out of the hotel. Coat-tails flying, he raced up the main street and disappeared behind a building, while his cohorts set up a chant of derision.

Jones, furious at this turn in events, lit out after him, along with Frank Keller and George Bates, the Prospect blacksmith. Soon most of the men of the village were engaged in the man hunt. Bushy, a nineteen-year-old who was a good athlete, out-distanced his pursuers, but an inquisitive neighbor announced that she had seen the fugitive entering the back door of George Farley's house next to the cemetery.

The "posse" ran to the Farley house, where they found "Grandma" Farley, the oldest woman in the village, alone. Grandma knew nothing of the presence of a strange man in her house, but she let the men make a search. Keller found Bushy hiding under Grandma's bed. He dragged the fugitive out and Jones put handcuffs on the redhead, who was taken back to Squire Morris, who set bail at $500, a sum which the proprietor of the Union Hotel furnished. Bushy was taken to Utica Jail. The grand jury found him guilty of assault and battery on Jones and the judge sentenced him to thirty days in jail.

But, like the pussy-willows, Joe came back to Hinckley in the spring, where he crouched behind the bat and heckled batters from opposing teams as if nothing had happened. It took more than thirty days in the "cooler" to calm down the ubiquitous redhead.

WHAT'S IN A NAME?

Several times each year, motorists stop citizens in Prospect and ask, "Are we in Barneveld?" And the Prospecters, though hardly flattered by the question, will patiently explain that the motorists passed through Barneveld on their way to Prospect. "But that was Trenton," the tourists will argue. "The signs said so."

Prospect folks used to go into lengthy explanations of how Trenton became Barneveld though it still remained Trenton, but the younger generation merely shrugs its collective shoulders and says to the baffled motorists, "You figure it out," the reason for such callousness being that they can't understand it themselves.

The story goes back over a century and a half. Gerrit Boon, who was founding settlements for the Holland Land Company, established one called Oldenbarneveld at the junction of the Cincinnati and Steuben Creeks, and another about eighteen miles north, which he wished to name Kortenaer but which was eventually called Boonville after its founder.

As BIJAH would have said, "Things swashed along pretty well" for a while, until the residents of Oldenbarneveld evidently found that name too much of a mouthful, so they changed it to Trenton, and as Trenton it endured for over three quarters of a century. Boonville, evidently satisfied with its name, stood pat.

The town and village of Trenton celebrated their 100th anniversaries in 1898-1899 with pageants, dinners and oratory. Continual reference to the Dutch heritage and to John of Barneveld stirred up a mild hornets' nest in Trenton, which was feeling dissatisfaction because much of its mail was going to other Trentons throughout the Union. As one woman wrote: "One of the misfortunes incident to the rapid growth of our country was that names could not be found fast enough, and so the same one was used over and over again, but it seemed stupid to have repeated Trenton when the village already had such a good and grand name as Barneveld."

Others felt the same way, so a petition was circulated in the village and enough names procured to get the post office and the railroad station changed from Trenton to Barneveld. Changing the village name had to go before the voters in March, 1903, and the advocates of the new—or was it old?—name thought they were in.

Boonville caught the name-changing fever. An intellectual society decided that Kortenaer, the name Boon had originally selected, should become the new name of that village.

Opposition came from all sides, but chiefly from former residents of the two villages. Letters poured in to the newspapers, two from as far away as Des Moines, Iowa and Fort Collins, Colorado. Barneveld protests came from the descendants of Dr. Luther Guiteau and John H. Billings, the first two postmasters of that village. A man from Port Leyden accused the home folks of trying to name the village after a Dutch traitor, to which the Unitarian minister replied indignantly that John of Barneveld had been a patriot.

Boonville was also having its troubles. A man from Utica wrote: "If the name of our village is really so verdant that it has become necessary for the antiquaries to dig up a name, why not go down to the roots and appropriate the name of Eden, Nod or Babel? It would take a music critic to tell wherein Kortenaer had an advantage over Boonville in translucent, mellifluous euphony, and withal a word which no one but a scholarly, native-born Dutchman could ever learn to pronounce correctly."

George Worden, the wag from Prospect who wrote for the *Utica Daily Press,* annoyed the pro-Barneveld faction by suggesting, "If Trenton be changed to Barneveld, why not Vongobelgrecht for Holland Patent and Honyarikrupfttenheiden for Prospect? Just for a moment think of an honest Welshman by the name of Jones with a cold in his head, trying to say Barneveld." He signed his letter "Christian Van Burghlaer Ungelmier."

As the fateful election day approached, the Unitarian Church bell pealed merrily, for advocates of the change evidently had support from that quarter. The people of Trenton voted 55 to 34 to keep that name for their village, whereupon the bell came out of the Unitarian tower and was moved to the old Presbyterian Church, then the Grange Hall. The victors held a celebration in the hall in July. About 250 people sat down to a feast and danced throughout the evening.

The Kortenaerites evidently saw the hand-writing on the wall. The proposed change of name never came before the voters of Boonville.

THE VALUABLE COAT

Lewis Francis of Ava, a half-breed who spent his winters trapping animals and making baskets, landed in Boonville one Saturday evening in April, 1902, to sell his produce and to light up the village. He visited several saloons and was in a genial mood when he arrived at the taxidermist's shop of A. M. Church to dispose of his pelts.

Church had done business with Lewie before, and was acquainted with the half-breed's craving for "red-eye." He got a whiff of the Ava man's breath as he examined the pelts. When the transaction had been completed, Church said, "Here's $46.75, Lewie. You got some money in your pocket?"

Lewie produced a few bills and some change.

"Good," said Church. "I'll put this money in an envelope and seal it. You stick it in your inside coat pocket and don't you dare touch it until you get home."

Lewie tucked the envelope into the pocket of his ragged garment, thanked Church, and started out to do the village. He sampled liquor at every bar and had a real jolly time. By eleven o'clock he could hardly walk and his mind could hold only one thought—a place to spend the night. He tried to camp on the porch of Eli McClusky at the corner of Bridge and Charles Streets at the lower end of the village, but McClusky shewed him away, telling him his house was not a hotel and that there were several of them in the village. He suggested that Lewie try one.

Lewie did not act too happy about this development, for he was getting doggoned sleepy. The red-eye had warned up his innards and he felt hot and sweaty, so he took off his coat and hung it over a hitching post on the opposite side of Bridge Street and continued his wanderings, which carried him toward the center of the village.

The next morning, Henry McClusky, who lived on First Street, went to his henhouse to collect eggs. Much to his surprise, he found a bird of another feather, for on the floor lay Lewie, stretched out on his back and snoring loudly. McClusky woke up the half-breed, whom he knew well, and asked him why he was roosting with the chickens.

Lewis sat up, rubbed his eyes and looked around. His mind was a blank. He didn't even remember trying to sleep on Eli McClusky's porch.

"Where's my coat?" he asked Henry McClusky.

"What coat?"

Lewie scrambled to his feet. "My coat!" he cried. "Church put my money in an envelope in the pocket and told me not to touch it until I got home." He raced out to look for his garment.

He hammered on tavern doors, rousing sleepy bartenders who knew nothing about the coat. He stopped pedestrians and pleaded with them to help him to find his coat.

In the meantime, sedate Boonville citizens on their way to and from church, got quite a laugh out of a ragged coat which was draped over a hitching post on Bridge Street. One man poked it with his cane and said laughingly to his wife that the garment looked pretty valuable.

Lewie, after a desperate but unsuccessful search, wended his footsteps toward Ava, cold sober but leaden of heart. All of his earnings had disappeared with the coat.

Late that Sunday afternoon, Miss Carrie Talcott, sister-in-law of Henry McClusky, decided to call on Mrs. Walter Franklin, the daughter of Eli McClusky. As she wandered down Bridge Street, she spied the coat hanging over the hitching post.

She said to Eli McClusky, "I think that's a valuable coat hanging on the post across the street. It doesn't look like much, but it may be worth over forty dollars." She winked at Eli.

He took the hint, for he had helped to search for Lewie's garment that morning. He came back with the coat. Sure enough, Lewie's money rested in the pocket where Church had placed it the evening before. Most of Boonville had seen the coat, but Miss Talcott was the only one who had connected the garment with Lewie. She took the coat and money home and on Monday morning sent word to Lewie to come and get his property.

Lewie must have run every step of the way, for he was out-of-breath when he arrived to claim his coat and to vow never again to leave his valuable garment hanging over a hitching post where any person in Boonville might pick it up.

WELSH CONFUSION

The Welsh settlers in the Adirondack foothills suffered from a scarcity of given names. Celtic names such as Hugh, Evan and Owen were common, as were Biblical names like John, David and Thomas. It was common for a son to be named after his father: my great-grandfathers were Meredith H. Meredith and Thomas J. Thomas. And the Welsh, like the Scotch and Irish, had a system for indicating that the son was carrying his father's name. Instead of using "Mac" as in MacLean or "O" as in O'Brien, the Welsh showed the relationship by using "Ap." A boy named Hugh ap Hugh might become Hugh Pugh; again, Richard ap Richard could become Richard Prichard.

This similarity of names in communities that were predominately Welsh offered no little confusion, so a series of nicknames was devised to distinguish a Williams or a Jones or a Roberts. These nicknames were derived from the place in Wales from which the man had emigrated, from the spot where he lived, from his trade, or from some peculiarity of his character.

In the early days, men were distinguished by their place of emigration. Two of the stone houses still standing are *Pen-morva,* built by Robert Thomas on the road from Remsen to Starr Hill, and *Llanbadarn Fawr,* off the lower road from Prospect to Remsen, built by William Lewis.

The Welsh around Remsen often were distinguished one from another by the place where they lived. One family might be Jones Farm, another Evans Stone House, or, as in the case of the Griffiths family, who lived in a red house, Davy *Ty Coch* and Owen *Ty Coch.* Two men bearing identical names were known as Hugh Flat Hughes and Hugh Swamp Hughes, while Richard Roberts was called Dick Sixty because he lived at Sixty Acres.

Tradesmen were often singled out from one another. John Buzzsaw Jones ran a sawmill and lumberyard in Remsen; Bill Tinman Roberts made tinware up near Pen Y Craeg chapel; Bill Painter Jones plied his trade in Prospect. Holland Patent had its Dick Buttermilk Jones and Remsen its Dick Crowbar Jones.

The most picturesque nicknames grew from a man's character or from some peculiar thing he had done. William Williams of Remsen, a mason with a sunny disposition, once swallowed a lathnail while laughing. Ever afterward, he was known as Billy Lathnail. Over in Prospect, lived Robert Hughes, a little man who wore a red wig and liked to sit on the steps of the general store eating bananas. He was dubbed *Robin Coch,* or red robin, while his tiny wife was affectionately referred to as the Wren. A man who worked at the Prospect quarry was known as Earring John, for he wore gold earrings to cure his rheaumatism, and another quarrier, who owned a ferocious bulldog, was known as Griff *Diawl* or Devil.

The most delightful character lived in the Welsh District above *Pen Y Caerau* chapel. Griffith Roberts was a farmer. One day he walked down the main street of Remsen, carrying a long stick. When asked what he planned to do with it, he announced that he was going to make a crooksled, so he forever afterward was known as Griff Crooksled. For some years he was unaware of his nickname but one day when he went in to pay his taxes, he found his name recorded as "Griff Crooksled" in the book.

"What a devil of a name to call a man," he complained.

Griff and his "old woman" never seemed to agree. One summer day, during the midst of a terrific thunderstorm, Griff sharpened his scythe and went out to mow hay over the protests of his wife.

"Griff," she cried from the doorway. "You'll get struck!"

As Griff told the story, "Mary was hollerin' on me to come in house. Lightnin' run like blue snake on sigh and took everything but handle but I kept sighing and cut nothing."

Griff loved horses. He talked to them as if they were children. One day he missed old Jack and found him up to his nose in a swamp near the Beaver Meadow Brook.

"Shame of you, Jack," Crooksled scolded the horse. "Be like that in the Beaver."

And the horse was so ashamed of himself that he climbed right out of the swamp.

MORE ABOUT DINGLE DANGLE

Dingle Dangle Jones gained fame as the hunter who refused to carry a compass and eventually disappeared between Jock's Lake and Snyder Lake. Nelson Jones of Remsen, who hunted and fished with Dingle Dangle at the age of fourteen, insists that the hermit from Steuben carried a compass on a shoe-string in his vest pocket but seldom consulted it, for he claimed that mineral deposits in the North Lake area made it unreliable.

John R. Jones—even Nelson doesn't know where the Dingle Dangle came from—lived near where the body works is now situated in Steuben. As a young fellow, he gained a reputation as a baseball pitcher, and threw one of the first curve balls to be seen in the Adirondack foothills. He held the job of postmaster in Steuben Valley for years, and also dabbled in the manufacture of home remedies. "J. R.'s Tincture" at twenty-five cents a bottle became a household necessity for Steuben farmers, who called him Dr. Jones. Dingle Dangle also liked oratory, and would walk to Floyd nearly every week to participate with a debating society in that village.

Dingle Dangle was a medium-sized man who sported a heavy mustache. An old portrait reveals an intelligent face and hands whose fingers had become knobbed from frequent contacts with baseballs.

While in the post office, Dingle Dangle spent considerable time trying to invent a machine to carry mail, but was never successful. His gunsight, which he never had patented, worked quite well and maybe it did bring the deer closer, as its inventor claimed.

He also prepared an oily substance to put on flies, and he invariably came home with a fine mess of trout. He also worked from time to time as a house painter, and got into quite a verbal hassle with the State of New York over the amount of money due him for re-decorating the state house at North Lake.

After his unsuccessful love affair, which evidently took place not too early in life, Dingle Dangle took more and more to the woods for consolation. In the fall he would suddenly announce, "By goss, I'm going up in the woods." Picking up his rifle, traps, etc., he would start off, practically forgetting about food. He would visit friends on the way, and housewives who felt sorry for him would contribute baked goods and other necessities, so that when he reached North Lake he usually had enough to keep him alive for months. That was not difficult, for he ate little and served less to guests.

For years he had no camp of his own, but merely used other shanties and leantos, as was the custom in those days. When he decided to build his own camp at North Lake, he went to Sand Lake, where a pile of lumber stood ready for a future camp builder, took a few boards each time, and eventually got enough to put up his own camp. He returned to Steuben Valley each spring, carrying the results of a winter's trapping, also a supply of spruce gum and jerked verison, which he distributed among the small boys.

Dingle Dangle evidently had no sense of direction. And he had the unfortunate habit of following woods roads which often led him far from his destination. Nelson Jones was with him on one occasion when, after wandering around through the forest for hours, they arrived at the spot from which they had started.

The day after election, when Dingle Dangle left Steuben Valley for his last trip to Snyder Lake, he told his friends, "By goss, I bring out some good fur for you this time—marten, maybe."

The hermit never had a camp at Snyder Lake, so he had probably decided to appropriate some other man's shack as a seat of operations for his winter's trapping. When he left Jock's Lake and the Adirondack League Club guides yelled at him that he was going in the wrong direction, the compass on a shoestring probably rested in his vest pocket. That fact can never be proved or disproved, for Dingle Dangle never reached Snyder Lake. He became part of the wilderness.

ALLIE

"The Bowery, the Bowery, I'll never go there any more." So sang Allie Phillips, who delivered the mail in Trenton Falls forty-odd years ago. Old timers remember Allie as a heavy-set, stooped man in perennial need of a shave. As his horse made its way up the road, folks would come out and chat with Allie and ask his opinion on a variety of subjects, knowing they would receive an answer that would amuse them.

When Mrs. Byron White first came to Trenton Falls, she stood admiring an adjoining field covered with yellow mustard blossoms as Allie drove up with the mail. She pointed to the flowers and asked if they had any value.

Allie took a squint at the field and drawled, "Never heard of mustard being any good except in a ham sandwich."

Allie liked anything that could be eaten. He was visiting with Sherm Moore one day. Sherm invited Allie to taste some new-fangled powdered milk he had purchased. Allie liked the milk so well that he downed the whole canful.

He frequented Charlie Morgan's store, for he liked to visit with the proprietor, who drove the livery to the railroad station and was a character in his own right. Charlie, who was quite a pal of John Barleycorn, would sway on the front seat of the surrrey with the canopy-fringed top. He boasted that he never missed meeting a train, though he usually made the morning one by a hair's breadth. "Never worry," he told his customers. "I've never missed a train yet." He did miss one morning train, to the consternation of a group of well-dressed ladies bound for a shopping tour of Utica.

Allie made a picturesque figure as he sat on the pickle barrel at Morgan's store, eating raw frankforts and crackers. He would buy a pound of franks, a pound of soda-crackers, and a pound of Ox-heart chocolates and sit there and eat them all for a little snack, while neighboring children stood around and marvelled at his appetite.

Allie was the son of S. A. Phillips, an early settler on the Russia side of the West Canada Creek. The father made butter tubs in a small mill on Adams Brook and at one time owned the houses now occupied by Clark Ogden and Yates Eckert. Allie lived in the Eckert house, where he raised a large family, did a little farming, carried the mail, and performed odd chores in Trenton Falls.

Young folks considered Allie "queer," so the mail-carrier often became the butt for practical jokers. Being a congenial soul, he enjoyed walking down the creek in the evening to chat with the maids who worked for the summer people. Wind of these excursions carried to the ears of a group of gay young blades, who decided to teach him a lesson. Allie was on his way home, singing "The Bowery," when a group pounced on him, poured molasses over him, decorated him with hens' feathers, and sent him home to his wife.

Allie, like most folks in small villages, liked to swap things. Gardie Parks, a shrewd character who lived about a half mile away from Phillips, sauntered over one day and asked Allie for some hay.

Allie, who was generous to a fault, waved his hand at a pile of hay and said, "Sure, Gardie, take what you want."

Gardie already had his eye on a wagon which was already loaded. "I'll take that along," said he.

Allie agreed, so Gardie drove off with the wagon loaded with hay. Gardie was rather absentminded in his own way, so he forgot to return the wagon, and Allie failed to miss it. Gardie had the wagon painted so that it shone like new. Allie came over to visit, admired the bright wagon, and bought it from Gardie.

Some time later, Allie had a craving for bees, so he jumped into the shiny wagon and drove over to see Gardie, who was an "expert" at raising bees. Allie pointed to a hive and asked to buy it.

"Will you swap the wagon for it?" asked Gardie.

Allie agreed readily, and staggered home with the hive to discover that it contained no bees.

THE BEDSIDE MANNER

Countryside doctors seldom pretended to be specialists. In fact, they pretended not at all. If they knew the trouble with the patient, they came out with the blunt truth, however hard it might be to take. They roamed through the foothills in every kind of weather, and went out on calls at all hours of day and night. In winter, they brought their snowshoes and a shovel, the better to cover the distance from the road to the farmhouse.

The best-known of the foothills doctors operated out of Remsen. Dr. George C. Morey had served in the Civil War and had practiced medicine in Grant, but he spent the major part of his career in Remsen and is always associated with that village.

A big, hulking, mustached man who dressed carelessly and was never known to wear a necktie, Doc drove his pair of bay horses through villages at break-neck speed. People who saw the cloud of dust would say, "There goes Doc Morey." He wore his glasses on his forehead and would lower them when compelled to read. Black cigars were his constant companions, and he lit them with matches he claimed "wouldn't go out in the wind." He chased down the taste of the strong cigars with cloves, which he ate by the pound. He was married three times, and outlived all his wives.

Doc Morey's two loves were horses and firearms. He usually drove the best pair of bays in Remsen and his house was a veritable arsenal. His pet hate was barking dogs. He carried a revolver with him on his tours of duty. If dogs harassed his horses, the doctor would shoot at them to scatter them. On one visit to a farm in Russia, he made the mistake of killing the family collie and had to fork up fifty dollars for his good marksmanship.

The revolver served him well on a trip to Wheelertown, where the patriarch of a family of woodsmen was taken seriously ill. Doc Morey drove up to see him and left some pills for the patient to take, saying he would return in the morning. Knowing that woodsmen had a superstitious aversion to medicine, he came back prepared for trouble. He got it. When he entered the house, the old man's henchmen were lined up waiting for him. The medicine had not cured the patient over night and the woodsmen were after the doctor's hide. Doc Morey calmly pulled out his revolver, covered the group, and backed out to his horse and buggy. The patient recovered.

Doc Morey would travel miles into the wilderness to save a life. French Louie broke through the ice on Brook Trout Lake and caught pneumonia. A trapper brought in word of Louie's plight, so Trume Haskell got the news to Doc Morey, who was then practicing in Grant. The doctor met Trume near Nobleboro and the pair drove as far as they could on snow-packed lumber roads. They left their team at a lumber camp and reached Louie's place on snowshoes. They stayed five days, alternately watching Louie and fishing for trout through the ice. "You'll be all right now, Louie," said the doctor in parting. He poohpoohed the idea of taking a fee, saying that he had had a fine vacation, but Louie dug into a box and brought forth fifty dollars which he insisted that the doctor take.

New-fangled sanitation ideas meant little to Doc Morey. In vaccinating a group of Remsen school children, he merely lined them up, wiped their arms in turn with the same dab of cotton saturated in alcohol, and jabbed each child with the same unsterilized needle. If a youngster yelped with pain, Doc merely growled at him and called him a sissy. There is no record of any of the children getting infection or smallpox from Doc's needle.

No man could be gruffer than Doc Morey, and young girls were scared to death of him, for he liked to give them playful squeezes when he entered a house. One young woman who enjoyed playing chronic invalid complained that she thought her liver was shrinking, whereupon the doctor addressed her by name and added, "Hell, you've got a liver bigger than an ox." The "invalid" lived to be nearly eighty, but she called Doc Morey only in times of extreme emergency.

When another woman tried to commit suicide by taking a dose of poison, Doc Morey used his best bedside manner.

"What in hell you been taking?" he asked her.

The woman told him. "I wanted to die," she whined.

Doc Morey frowned beneath his glasses and growled, "If you want to die, come over to my office and I'll give you something that will really kill you."

The woman lived, as did most of Doc Morey's patients. Maybe his bedside manner worked wonders.

LAURIE BACH

One of the delights of summers I spent in Prospect as a boy was Laura Worden, the widow of a Civil War veteran who lived next house to my grandmother. Though she was a buxom lady with a ready smile and a quick wit, our folks referred to her as Laurie Bach, the Welsh for Little Laura, the *bach* being a term of affection reserved for close relatives and dear friends.

Laura was one of several "Edwards girls" who had been raised near Pen Y Caerau chapel in the days when young ladies dabbled in embroidery and oil painting. One of the girls, Margaret Chase, became a professional and turned out set pieces of lilacs, roses, etc., which she sold at good prices. Laura, who was less ambitious, turned her talents to wilder things, such as animals and fish. I doubt if she ever tried to sell a painting. She would shrug and say, "I'm not good enough. Maggie is the artist in our family."

George Worden, her late husband, had been the one Democrat in a Republican community who could win elections and get appointments. He held the postmastership in his general store during the first Cleveland administration, and stuck to his political principles though outnumbered in any argument. He was proud that his family had been the first settlers in Prospect, and he left invaluable material about early days in the village. As a mere youth, he had enlisted in the Third New York Artillery and he later became one of the stalwarts of the local post of the G. A. R. His correspondence to the Utica papers was tinged with rural humor, and he found time to write amateur plays which were presented by local talent in the Walters Opera House.

To Laurie Bach, his chief claim to fame lay in his ability to catch fish. Whenever the day was right, he would close up his store and drive to Beaver Meadow Brook and return with strings of trout which seem fabulous. Laurie used to tell me about the day George came back with 60 speckled beauties. I had considerable faith in my friend's veracity, but I simply had to check this statement with my uncle, who promptly verified it.

Laurie's marriage to George probably dictated her choice of subject matter. Framed pictures of trout predominated in her collection—

still-life piles of speckled beauties, lone trout swimming in grassy brooks, and, above all, her last painting, a canvas which occupied nearly an entire wall. This picture struck my boyhood fancy. Against a background of stream and grassy banks, a large trout was jumping halfway out of the water to grasp a fly. His body shone with multi-colored radiance, and desperation seemed to grip him as he struggled to disgorge the fly and hook which were embedded in his upper lip. One thing was missing from the painting—the angler's line.

Boylike, I went fishing nearly every day, and I would share my meagre catch with Laurie, for I knew that the gift of trout not only pleased her but brought back memories.

It was some time before I screwed up courage to ask Laurie why she had never painted in the fisherman's line.

She looked at me wistfully and said, "It is years since I have touched a brush. My hands are too old. The line needs a steady hand, and I no longer have it." She smiled and added "Some day that painting will be yours. I promise you that." And I went home, thrilled to the bone.

I kept track of Laurie during the winters through correspondence with my aunt. "Laura is tatting, as usual," would come the word; and one Christmas my mother received a beautiful handkerchief with a border containing the old lady's handiwork.

As Laurie's life neared the close, my folks kept close tabs on her. One February night, when the wind whistled down the chimneys and snow nearly buried the village, my uncle became concerned about his neighbor. Her lamp was still lit in the morning, so he waded through the drifts to her door. When he entered, there sat Laurie Bach, both feet in the oven, singing a Welsh hymn at the top of her voice. "I felt that God was with me during the storm," she told him.

The inevitable summer came when I could no longer visit Laurie. The unfinished painting had vanished along with her other household goods. I never learned what became of it, but I think I know why she never painted in the fisherman's line. Memories of her husband would always still her hand.

V. MURDER

The Adirondack foothills have been singularly free from serious crime over the years, a tribute to the character of the inhabitants. During the 1880's, however, four rather sensational murders made the front pages of the newspapers. Three of them were solved and the murderers were punished, but the fourth still remains a mystery.

The known murderers were men with diseased minds: a priest whose insanity drove him from his pastorate and caused him to spur his imbecile brother to kill a man; a Civil War veteran who was unable to adjust himself to civilian life; a German immigrant who struck down his friend in a fit of rage.

The fourth murderer, who was never apprehended, killed a man in a robbery which netted him less than four dollars.

A MAD CLERIC

Rev. John Craven came to Constableville about 1875 as the parish priest of St. Mary's Church. He was at loggerheads with his parishioners from the start, and protests were sent to the Bishop of Ogdensburg about Craven's heavy drinking, also about his religious fanaticism which bordered on insanity. The Bishop investigated the case, with the result that Craven was deposed from his sacred office.

The unfrocked priest remained in the village, where he lived with his mother, an imbecilic sister and a powerful brother, Patrick, whose brain did not compare with his brawn.

Rev. J. A. MacKenna was sent to Constableville to replace Craven, and a few years after his arrival, the church burned to the ground. Father McKenna set about raising funds for a new church, which was to be constructed nearer the heart of the village.

John Craven immediately threw a block in his path. He claimed that he was still the legitimate priest of the parish, and when Father MacKenna and the parishioners attempted to take foundation stones from the site of the burned church to use them for the new building, Craven and his brother guarded the stones and refused to let them be removed.

The Catholics of Constableville retaliated by making life miserable for the Cravens. They cut off the tail of John's horse; they cut his harness and buffalo robes to pieces; they set fire to his winter's supply of wood.

The Cravens did not take these acts in stride. They spread such terror throughout the village, that citizens were afraid to go abroad nights for fear of being butchered. John Craven claimed that the Protestants had lent him a room, which he would use until he rebuilt his church on the site where it had burned.

John Craven, under persecution from the villagers, began to do some strange things. He claimed Father MacKenna was an imposter, and that he would get Senator Kernan of Utica for counsel and show up MacKenna's "clique of robbers." He also wrote to Secretary of State Blaine and requested $70,000 of the Treasurer of the State of New York with which to rebuild his church.

Affairs in Constableville were not going too smoothly. The Cravens, powerful fellows with bull necks and red complexions, began to fight with the people. Pat struck a brewery owner and John pitched into John Doyle when the latter tried to take away stone for the foundation of the new church.

This last attack brought the case to a head in September, 1881. Doyle swore a warrant for the arrest of John for the assault, which had taken place in June. John, sensing that the warrent had been issued to keep him from guarding the stone, retreated to the cemetery, where he and Pat armed themselves with scythe blades and dared the constable to come in and arrest them.

The village president and trustees appeared, accompanied by most of Constablevile. John told them he was willing to be arrested if some person was put in charge of the property so the stones would not be "stolen."

At this point, Barney Egan, an elderly citizen who had been imbibing rather freely, arrived at the cemetery gate. He looked over the situation and asked, "Why don't you arrest them? I can arrest them both alone."

John Craven said, "Come in, Barney, and welcome."

Egan picked up a stick and advanced with a threatening gesture. "I helped put them stones there," he said, "and I mean to have them."

"Go for him, Pat," said John to his brother, "and drive him out."

Pat responded with a will. His scythe flashed back and forth several times, tearing Egan to pieces. Blood showed through his shirt from three horrible gashes on his back; his left ear was sliced off, also two toes of his left foot; the flesh was hewn from his left arm until the bone showed. Blood fairly spurted from his body as he fell to the ground.

The crowd stood there, stunned. Not a man made a move to help Egan. John drew himself to his full height and announced that he had won a victory for the church and for the British crown. He, followed by Pat and the mother, went home.

Egan died three hours later and the three Cravens were arrested. The coroner's jury brought a verdict of murder in the first degree against Patrick Craven, aided and comforted by his brother. They were taken to Lowville jail to await action by the Grand Jury.

The two Cravens proved to be unruly prisoners. Each night they kept up an infernal yelling and screaming. It was found necessary to put the brothers in separate cells. John made one attempt to escape but the jailor quieted him with a blow over the head with a club. The ex-priest also tried to keep a knife after a meal but it was taken away from him.

The Lowville Fair was in progress, and it proved less popular to the visitors than the Cravens, for countless people visited the jail each day to get a look at the prisoners.

The trial took place on October 7, and it must have been bewildering to the judge and jury. Patrick was such an imbecile that he could not answer the simplest questions. John also refused to make any direct answers. Instead, he produced sheafs of papers which seemed pointless to the court. Senator Kernan had refused to defend the brothers, whereupon Thomas S. Jones of Boonville was assigned as counsel for the defense. Jones put in a plea of insanity, and the case was referred to a commission of three to investigate.

The commission reported on November 11 that they found both Cravens to be insane. John did not take kindly to the report and he interrupted proceedings so often that Judge Merwin let him have the floor.

John said he was addressing the crowd "in the name of the people of the United States, the Catholic church and the British crown." He claimed that he "represented the British lion on American soil." He got so excited that he pulled off his coat and waved his arms around his head and shouted at the top of his voice. The constable had to put an end to the harangue. The brothers were taken back to jail and then committed to a hospital for the criminally insane.

This unfortunate affair cast a pall over Constableville, but Father MacKenna and his flock continued their work of building the new church—from the foundations of the old one—and on June 26, 1884, the Right Reverend Bishop Wadham of Ogdensburg accepted the church on behalf of the pastor.

DARK NIGHT IN NORTH WESTERN

Herb Paddock, captain of a state scow on the Black River Canal, paid off his six-man crew at the Bull's Head, about four miles above North Western, one Friday afternoon in November, 1883. The men pocketed their wages, and five of them rejoiced at anticipation of pleasures they would enjoy over the weekend.

Not so Robert Davis, a 55-year-old bachelor from Webster Hill over Steuben way. Davis didn't enjoy drinking at bars, nor did he care to fight. It was true that he had been challenged by a fellow boatman named Adams the week before, and the pair had gone into a field to settle the difficulty. Cooler heads had prevented fisticuffs, much to the relief of Davis.

The scow reached Hillside late in the afternoon. Davis, having been paid $35, jumped off to see Mike Hogan, who ran a grist and saw mill there. Mike wasn't at home, but his wife, a buxom dame dressed in a yellow calico dress almost covered with a blue apron, stood talking with Isaiah Van Dewalker, the lock-tender.

Davis handed Mrs. Hogan a twenty-dollar bill, saying, "I gave your husband ten last month and this will make it thirty. Keep it till I call for it."

Mrs. Hogan took the money and Davis hurried for the scow, his body bent forward and his hat down over his eyes.

Van Dewalker took a few puffs on his clay pipe and asked, "He owe your old man money?"

Mrs. Hogan's black eyes twinkled through her spectacles. "Not Davis," she said. "He has my husband hold money for him from time to time. Guess he's afraid somebody will steal it, for he never spends much."

The scow pulled up outside North Western for the weekend. Frank Buckley and Ichabod Webster planned to do the taverns in the village, while Adams, out for greater excitement, hopped a ride on a beer wagon headed for Rome. Davis started for North Western but stopped on the towpath. Webster, who had been raised on Webster Hill and had known Davis all his life, asked the trouble.

"I haven't got my pocketbook," replied Davis, fishing in his overalls pockets. "I think I must have left it down at Hogan's. Maybe I better go after it."

Frank Buckley stuck his head out of a window and threw Davis' pocketbook to the towpath. "You left it in your bunk, Bob," he said with a laugh.

Davis went off with his shambling gait, chuckling to himself and shaking his head at his own absent-mindedness.

Buckley and Webster met him later at Starr's Hotel. He also was seen at the Half Way House about nine o'clock. He had nothing to drink in either place. His last stop was with James Reese, the cobbler, whom he paid twenty-five cents he owed him.

The day had been rainy, and the ensuing night was damp and exceedingly dark. Marcus Van Buskirk, who passed the state scow late in the evening, met a strange man, to whom he spoke but who did not answer. Van Buskirk also thought he saw the man peeking through a window of the scow. A short time later, Archibald Plato, Dick Macomber and Charles Gue saw a stranger on the bridge near the scow. They also spoke to him but received no reply.

Buckley and Webster found things dull in North Western, so they started for the scow around ten thirty, feeling their way carefully through the pitch dark night. Buckley heard someone breathing. Though he stopped short, his foot struck something soft and he nearly sprawled in the towpath. It was the body of a man, lying face down in the mud.

Webster ran to the scow for a lantern. Its glow showed that the form which lay sprawled on the ground was that of their boatmate, Bob Davis. The man's back was dry, indicating that he had been struck from behind and had not moved since the fall. Blood was clotted in his hair behind the right ear. His pocketbook was gone!

The two men became panic-stricken. Buckley ran pell-mell to the hotel, while Webster got Dr. R. H. Hews out of bed and rushed him to the scene.

News of the assault was soon village property. When Webster got back to the scene with the doctor, any incriminating footprints or wheel marks had been obliterated. Davis was sitting on a stool in the scow's cabin.

Dr. Hews examined the great bruise behind Davis' right ear and asked him how he got it. Davis, always a man of slow speech, was too groggy to reply intelligently. The only word that came through clearly was "smacked," indicating that he had been hit by someone. The doctor treated the wound and Davis motioned that he wanted his shoes taken off so he could lie down on his bunk. This was done, and the doctor stayed all night, applying cold applications to his head and warm water to his feet.

Davis got no better, so Dr. H. G. Reed of Westernville bled him the next morning. Reed announced that the injury had been inflicted by a stone or some flat instrument, for it was more of a bruise than a cut. At four-thirty in the afternoon, Davis died.

Fingers were pointed in the direction of Adams, who had quarreled with Davis the previous week. A constable rode down to Delta, where he encountered a friend of Adams who swore that Adams was so drunk in Delta Saturday night that he "could not have vanquished a lamp post in a hand-to-hand encounter."

Van Buskirk and the three men who had met the stranger on the bridge could have been of help, but none of them could offer any kind of description of the man who had been so unsociable to them.

The villagers were so horror-stricken that no family would take the body of Davis into a home. It lay in the bunk of the scow while the coroner's inquest was held at the Half Way House. The jury decided that "Davis came to his death from being hit by an instrument in the hands of some person to the jury unknown."

Davis' brother came to identify the body. The scow was towed to the village and the remains taken out on the towpath, where a post mortem examination was made by the two doctors.

Robbery seemed to be the only motive for the murder, unless Davis had some enemy unknown to his boatmates. Some people thought the attack had been aimed at Captain Paddock, who had received between $100 and $125 as wages for himself and wife, who did the cooking for the men. That theory had a serious fallacy, for the captain was erect of carriage and lively in his movements, whereas Davis slouched along with his hat over his eyes.

If Davis was the intended victim, the robber and murderer made out rather badly. In addition to the $20 Davis had given to Mrs. Hogan, he had paid Paddock $6 for board and had mailed $5 to a brother in Boonville. A life was taken for less than four dollars, for David, on that Saturday night, had spent thirty cents in addition to the quarter he had paid Reese.

LOCK 66

At one o'clock on a June afternoon in 1887, Irving E. Jackson, a farmer who lived two miles down the Black River Canal below Boonville, stirred up a cloud of dust as he drove up to the home of Constable Thomas L. Hart. Minutes later, he and the law officer raced madly out of the village, followed by Justice A. L. Hayes, Ex-Deputy Kilkenny, Canal Superintendent Pete Phillips and Dr. G. F. English.

They found a cluster of awe-stricken natives below Lock 66. In the water, partly covered by debris, lay the body of a young woman. She had been stabbed in the breast and abdomen and her blood reddened the brown water.

On the bridge below stood an old, bearded man, his arms wrapped around a golden-haired, two-year-old boy. Tears streamed down the man's face and his body shook with sobs. When Hart asked him where the murder had been committed, he pointed to the towpath and said, "There, and by my son."

A woman pushed her way through the crowd. "It's Josie Rosa-Cross," she cried. "It's Josie, sure enough, it's her."

"Where's your son?" Hart asked the old man.

"He ran into the woods," replied the latter, pointing.

Hart and Kilkenny started after the murderer. They did not have to travel far, for a thick-set man of 35 with unshaven face and a scraggy mustache came out of the woods near the scene. Phillips asked him if he had a revolver. The man shook his head. He handed Hart a pen-knife and a jack-knife.

"Did you kill her?" snapped Hart.

The man shrugged. "I don't remember."

"He killed her," cried the old man. "He didn't want her to go back to her mother, so he stabbed her with a butcher knife. He held her with his left arm and stuck the knife into her breast several times. When she fell, he stabbed her in the belly."

Hart turned to the prisoner. "What's your name?" he asked.

"Clement Arthur Day. I don't feel bad about it. I have lived long enough and so had she."

Hart took him to the Boonville lockup, where he was handcuffed and placed in a rear cell. Dr. English had the body of Josephine Rosa-Cross brought to the Bateman & McClusky undertaking rooms.

Though the old man smelled of "red-eye," he was able to talk. His son, a widower, had appeared at Lock 66, which the old man tended, shortly after the canal had opened in the spring. The twenty-one-year-old Josie had lived with him there for weeks, though the pair were not married. They had left for a time, but had returned the night before the murder. Josie had found a note from her mother, pleading with her to come back to Coonrad.

That morning, Josie wrote to her mother and started for Boonville to mail the letter. The old man watched her and Day walk along the towpath. He saw his son stab her and throw the body into the lock. Frightened, he picked up the small boy and bolted himself inside the lockhouse.

His son cried, "I want you to come down and help me get away with this body and bury it."

The old man refused. "You have killed her," he said, "and you will have to get away with the body the best you can."

He saw his son wash the blood off the stones with a tea kettle of water and take the body out of the lock.

"I've carried her across the sluice and hid her in some bushes," the son told him. "They'll get me and hang me. I'll have to get away from here." He saw his son disappear into the woods.

No previous crime had ever stirred Boonville as did this one. Crowds filed through the undertaking rooms all the next day to get a glimpse of the murdered woman's body.

Day acted cool at the inquest. He told how he had served in the Civil War with an Ohio regiment and admitted that during most of his life he had been a wanderer. His wife had died two years before, leaving him with a boy of ten who was working on the canal, and the little tot, whom Day claimed was the son of his wife and his brother. He did not deny committing the crime. He seemed pleased when he was taken to Ready's photography shop for photographs.

Hundreds of men gathered at the Boonville depot when the evening train for Utica pulled in. Day, handcuffed, was escorted through a crowd which cried, "Hang him!" and "Rope!" On the train, he showed his only touch of emotion. In speaking of his ten-year-old son, he said, "Poor little fellow. He'll feel awful when he finds we ain't there."

The train also carried the body of Josie, and the old man and the little boy, who were being taken to Rome.

While Day awaited trial, the histories of him and Josie Rosa-Cross were fitted together. His tale turned out to be substantially true, except that he had maimed his brother with an axe. Josie's story turned up some interesting facts. Josie, a pretty, light blonde girl, gave music lessons in McConnellsville until she was seduced by the sheriff, a married man. Her child died, but her reputation was ruined. She and her mother moved to Lee, where Josie married a 19-year-old youth, Frank Cross, without her mother's consent.

The day after the marriage, she and Cross went hop-picking in Waterville, where he came down with typhoid fever. She nursed him back to health and then went back to her mother.

The two women moved to Coonrad. One day they needed stove polish, so they stopped Day, who lived in a nearby shack, and asked him to get them some. He complied, and he also sawed some wood. Josie seemed fascinated by Day, and despite her mother's protests, ran away with him.

Mrs. Rosa had been trying for some time to locate her daughter, so she consulted a clairvoyant in Utica and was told that Josie was living at Lock 66 on the Black River Canal near Boonville and that something dreadful was going to happen to her. The mother dispatched the letter which Josie had received the night before her death.

Day's trial was held in Rome in December, with Judge Williams presiding. Day appeared clean-shaven, dressed in a dark suit, a low-collared shirt and a blue tie. He alternately gazed around the room or rested his head on his hand. He showed no interest in answering questions.

His lawyer's plea of insanity did not sway the judge or jury. Day was convicted of murder in the first degree. When the judge asked Day if he wanted to be sentenced then or the next week, the prisoner said, "You have had enough of me. Go on and hang me. I'll take it now, the sooner the better." The judge sentenced him to be hanged on February 9, 1888.

Day enjoyed life in the Utica jail. He ate heartily and he slept well. He received countless letters from well-meaning people, asking him to repent. The sheriff was deluged with requests from curiosity-seekers who wished to witness the execution.

Day received a few visitors. The old man came with the little boy. Day said, "I want to die so that I can go to Josie." After the visit, Day laughed and remarked, "The old man shed crocodile tears, but he put it on. He was drunk again." The ten-year-old son, whom Day evidently loved, also came, and Day gave him to a farmer in Westmoreland.

Day enjoyed his last evening. He sang, danced, and played his guitar. He also imitated the crowing of a rooster and boasted of relations he had enjoyed with women in prison. He ate a hearty meal at midnight and fell into a deep sleep. For breakfast, he downed ham and eggs, fried potatoes, toast and strong coffee. Afterward, he thrummed on his guitar.

The execution was set for ten o'clock. Day dressed carefully. He wore a suit of black diagonal, sack coat, high collar and plain black tie. His watch chain was fastened to his vest with a red ribbon and a yellow rose graced his buttonhole.

Only twelve invitations had been issued to the general public, though the jury and law officers were there. As the procession started to cross the yard from the jail to the barn where the hanging was to take place, the sheriff slipped on the ice and fell. Day laughed loudly and reached down and helped the officer to his feet.

He mounted the scaffold with firm steps and insisted on helping the executioner place the knot under his chin. When all was ready, he turned to Deputy Burke, grasped his hand, kissed him and said good bye.

In March, an old man was seen walking down John Street in Cincinnati, Ohio. A chubby, golden-haired boy in a plaid dress toddled along beside him. The old man was puffing on a five-cent cigar he had been given at a nearby saloon. The tot also held a cigar between his lips and was blowing smoke toward the sky. They created considerable amusement for Cincinnati folks before the police stepped in, arrested old man Day—for it was he—and took the boy to a home for children.

Mrs. Ada M. Rosa, mother of the murdered girl, had complained of a bad heart in 1887 and was sure she would immediately follow her daughter to the grave. She died twenty-four years after the murder at Lock 66.

CEDAR JOHN

John Kienlen, known as Cedar John, lived in a shack near Stittville for over twenty years. A small French-Canadian, he raised potatoes and onions and sold them to his neighbors. He also did odd jobs for farmers.

Cedar John, a fifty-year-old bachelor, lived alone, but another unmarried man, a fifty-two-year-old German named Fritz Lipe, liked to shack up with the Canadian. This arrangement displeased Cedar John, for he felt that Lipe abused his hospitality.

One Saturday in July, 1887, John helped Dave Davis of Floyd take in some hay. When he got back to Stittville, he bought a quart of whiskey at the hotel and drank until he thought it time to go to bed, for when John got drunk, he became loud-mouthed and disagreeable.

Mrs. John McDermott, who lived across the road, saw the German go into John's shack about five thirty.

John headed for home about eleven o'clock. Simon Purtell's light was on, so the little man went up the steps. When Purtell came out, John offered him a drink which Simon refused. The Canadian sat down on the step to rest and to air his troubles before his neighbor. Purtell, who liked John, suggested that he go home to bed, and he smiled to himself as he heard John singing a French song as he disappeared in the darkness.

The McDermotts also saw John go home. They heard him trying to get into his shack, which evidently was locked.

"The old so-and-so is here," they heard John complain. "The old thief. The old liar. Give all your money to the women and have none left."

A light was put on in the shack and John evidently entered. Loud quarreling was heard in a foreign language, both by the McDermotts and by Gurden Price and William Blust, two young fellows on their way home after an evening in Stittville. A thud as of a falling body was heard before the light went out. The young men kept going, but the McDermotts, who were evidently curious folks, saw a man come out of John's shack and head for Fred Yop's place about eighty rods away.

Yop was drunk when Lipe came to his house to spend the night.

"Cedar has called me names and driven me out of his shack," Lipe complained. "No one can live with Kienlen when he's drunk. He's a pig."

"Why didn't you do something about it?" asked Yop.

"I guess I did," Lipe replied.

John McDermott, hearing no sounds from John's shack the next morning, walked over and peeked through the window. He saw John curled up on the bed against the wall and assumed that the Canadian was sleeping off his drunkenness. Later, he encountered Lipe, who said John's face had been bloody when he came home. This fact did not check with what Simon Purtell knew, so the two men broke into John's shack about five and found John lying face-down on the bed. He had partly disrobed, for his coat and vest and one shoe lay on the floor. A pool of blood stained the planks near the bed. McDermott turned John over. Blood still trickled from a deep gash over his right eye and another on the back of his head. He had been dead for hours.

Lipe had visited in the village that day. He not only told McDermott that he and John had had a row, but he went over to Anthony Huber's to air his grievances.

"Why didn't you lick him?" asked Anna, Huber's daughter.

"I guess he won't need any more licking," Lipe answered.

Coroner Myron W. Hunt ruled "That the said John Kienlen came to his death by injuries inflicted upon him by Frederick Lipe by means of a deadly weapon held in the hands of said Lipe."

A search that night failed to uncover the weapon, but Jim Owens found a hatchet the following morning in a small barn near John's shack. It was covered with blood and hair. Owens recognized it as one which had belonged to John.

Lipe, when arrested, pleaded not guilty to murder in the second degree. At his trial in Rome, Lipe interrupted Judge Williams to say in broken English, "No, I did not kill him." He was judged guilty by the jury, though some of the evidence was circumstantial, and Judge Williams sentenced him to hard labor in Auburn prison for life.

In April, 1889, Stittville citizens petitioned for the release of Lipe, for they felt that John had been more to blame than the German, but nothing came of it. A few months later, John's shack near the railroad burned down.

VI. NORTH WOODS

I sing a song of long departed days,
When hunters, trappers, hermits, lumberjacks,
Roamed through the virgin forest, packs on backs,
And spun tall tales before the campfire's blaze.
They hauled in speckled trout with skillful plays
Of rod and line and reel; and as for bears,
These dauntless hunters faced them in their lairs,
And brought them to their deaths in thrilling ways.

I never knew the men who wove these tales,
Nor do I vouch for any statement made.
I've told them once again before they fade
Forever in the forests, streams and dales.
For truth in them I hope you will not seek.
Just read them as I wrote them—tongue in cheek.

WHY GUGUGLE LAKE WENT DRY

Saturday evening brought the usual gathering to Dave Jones' store in Northwood. George Dolly sat tilted back with his feet against the pot-bellied stove, its iron sides cold on this summer night. Johnny Jones and the Kennedy brothers lolled against the counter and nodded their heads sympathetically as Pappy Tucker, who had cashed his pension check, profaned the smoke-laden air with a condemnation of the stinginess of the government toward Civil War veterans.

Pappy ran out of epithets and headed for Phil Smith's saloon to drown some of his sorrow, and Pete Hoffman, the miller, was lecturing on the superiority of coal oil over raw pork for horse colic, when who should walk in but G. B. L.

The appearance of the lanky, scraggy woodsman produced a wink or two from the gathered men, who settled themselves comfortably, knowing that G. B.'s wind-blown yarns usually were strung out longer than a taffy-pull.

G. B. settled himself on the counter between the dried apple barrel and the cracker box. He ignored the daggers Dave Jones was casting in his direction and he did not shiver in the stony silence which pervaded the store.

"Evening, men," he began. "Nice evening, ain't it?" Receiving no confirmation, he continued, "A night like this reminds me of one about nine years ago come next Tuesday. Something happened that night I've got to tell you about, and I've got to make it short, for I have a date in ten minutes.

"Me and Joe Boudle was fishing on Gugugle Lake up in the Adirondacks—"

"Gugugle Lake?" George Dolly interrupted. "There ain't no such place."

G. B. looked down his long nose at the heckler. "There ain't now," he admitted, "but there was nine years ago. As I was saying when I was rudely interrupted, me and Joe were fishing in Gugugle Lake. We'd had only fair to middling luck, only about eighty-five pound of trout after eight hours of fishing, and were getting ready to row to shore, when we both sat up straight in the boat.

"Coming from the woods, about a hundred rods from us, were the most ghostly yells and groans me and Joe ever heard. I'll admit I was sort of scared and Joe was whiter'n a sheet, but we put down our poles and Joe rowed hell-bent-for-election toward the shore." G. B. disappeared head first into the barrel and came up with a handful of dried apples. He munched one and asked, "Boys, what d'you suppose we found when we got to shore?"

Pete Hoffman rolled his chaw from cheek to cheek and scoffed, "Perhaps it was the ghosts of them there passel of wild cats that you strangled with a shoe-string over on Scudgaymudgey River last fall."

The guffaws which greeted this sally offended G. B., whose voice cracked with emotion as he went on, "Believe it or not, me and Joe found eighty-six Eyetalians lying, gaunt and wasted, piled six deep and nigh dead. They didn't have no more yaps left, but they told us through signs that they got lost in the woods and hadn't had a speck of food or a drop of water for a week.

"Well, to make a long story short, me and Joe carried all them Eyetalians down to Gugugle Lake and left 'em sucking like mad at the water while we run up into the woods to our camp to fetch the poor devils some vittles." G. B. selected two fat crackers and began to munch them.

Dave Jones couldn't refrain from asking what happened to the Italians, though he must have wanted to kick himself afterward.

G. B. beamed. "It was like this, gentlemen. When we got back with the venison, it was too late. There lay eighty-six Eyetalian corpses, all bloated with water. Me and Joe felt pretty bad about that, but we felt worse when we saw, instead of beautiful Gugugle Lake, a dark, deep mudhole. Good night, gentlemen, and thanks for listening."

G. B.'s footsteps had died away before his stunned audience came to its collective senses.

"You should have used a barrel-stave on him when he was upended in the barrel," George Dolly told Dave Jones.

A stranger who had dropped in to hear the yarn asked innocently, "And who was that fellow?"

"G. B.?" Dave Jones sputtered. "Don't you know him? He's G. B. L. or Gosh Blamed Liar. He lies so much he believes himself. Sometimes he lies so good we believe him until he gets away."

ROC HATED BEARS

Up Wilmurt way, folks say Roc Conklin lived on bear meat and bear blood. Some claim that the stocky hunter and trapper was half-bear, a theory Roc never denied, for he not only owned the biggest reputation as a bear-trapper in the West Canada Creek country, but he spun yarns that grew in length and incredulity with each re-telling.

Roc encountered bears morning, noon and night, and in three seasons of the year. He usually chased them, but occasionally they would tree him, a situation from which he extricated himself through one ruse or another. Roc could outwit any old bear. He killed one in the middle of a pond while battling it under water. He had his picture taken with four bears he had slaughtered in one day. Later, he regretted this photograph, for he felt sure he had killed at least ten bears on that historic occasion.

According to Roc, he was trudging along with his repeating rifle, loaded with five cartridges, slung over his shoulder. Five more cartridges rested in his coat pocket. He stopped short, for in the path ahead stood two of the biggest bears he had ever seen. They were swaying from side to side and sniffing the air. Roc, being a good man with a rifle, planted bullets between the eyes of the two bears so fast that both hit the ground at the same time.

The forest suddenly teemed with bears. They appeared from behind rocks, trees and bushes, all staring at the dauntless hunter. And Roc realized that he had interrupted a bear convention.

He killed the three largest bears and reloaded his rifle. The surviving animals, conscious that they were facing a fabulous hunter who gave no quarter, climbed trees and whined for mercy, but Roc dropped five of them from the treetops and grinned as he heard their bodies thud on the ground.

Though he sensed that he had broken all records with his kill of ten bears, Roc turned tail and ran for camp to get some more cartridges. On his return, there wasn't a bear in sight.

Despite this disappointment, Roc did not give up hunting bears. He had heard that the biggest bear ever to be seen in the West Canada Creek country was lurking in the woods behind Wilmurt, so he took to the trail, sure that this behemoth would fall before his trusty rifle. He climbed mountains, forded streams and fought his way through undergrowth, but at the day's end the bear had not put in an appearance, so Roc sat down on a hummock to rest before making the long journey home.

He reached into his pocket and produced a large piece of journey cake. Breaking it in two, he held a chunk in each hand and would bite first from the one and then from the other. As he put down his right hand, the biggest bear in the woods reached out and took a bite. Roc, surprised, withdrew that hand and put the other one down. The bear showed no partiality; it took a bite from that chunk of cake. And so the game went on, first Roc taking a bite of journey cake and then the bear. Roc would get a mouthful only to discover that the bear would also have one.

The journey cake got smaller and smaller, until only crumbs were left. When the last crumb fell to the ground, Roc made a dive for it, only to find that the bear had beaten him to it.

Roc really got worked up at this act of ingratitude. Forgetting all about his rifle, he kicked that durned bear so hard under the jaw that the biggest bear ever to be seen in the West Canada country ran whining into the forest. Roc picked up his rifle and started for home, which was in the opposite direction. He was so durned mad he had forgotten for once that he was bear hunting.

Roc's brother, Burt, could not approach Roc as a bear hunter, he being known as the Wilmurt expert on that elusive animal commonly called a fisher, though Burt preferred the more colloquial name of pekan.

As Roc told the story, he was helping Burt build a barn. They ran out of stone, so they agreed to meet at an old stone quarry three miles away at eight on a certain morning. Burt would take the team and a wagon, also a crowbar and an axe. Roc was to go on foot a little ahead of time and rid the territory of any bears, so he and Burt could break up enough stone for the foundation of the barn and haul it back to Burt's place.

Right after breakfast, Roc shouldered his rifle and took off. His wife called after him that he should take more shells in case he needed them. Roc, sure that the magazine was full, ignored her. He arrived at the rendezvous at eight to find that Burt had not put in an appearance, so he strolled around a bit and finally sat down on a knoll where he could survey the surrounding territory. Roc, the famous hunter, always made sure his back wasn't turned to a bear.

All of a sudden, a flock of partridges came flying toward him, acting as if scared to death. One lit near Roc, who took a few feathers off its breast with his rifle. He looked up to see a monstrous bear loping through the bushes toward him.

Roc said to himself, "Mr. Bear, you are my meat and I'm gonna take you out with me in Burt's wagon."

He raised his rifle and fired, but the bullet hit a sapling in front of the bear and split it cleaner'n a whistle.

The bear stopped, braced its front paws on the fallen sapling, and growled. Roc shot again and nearly took one of the bear's legs off. Down went the bear, rolling and rumbling and grabbing at its wounded leg with its mouth.

Roc knew he had his bear. He walked boldly to within feet of the animal, took careful aim, and pulled the trigger. Nothing happened! He worked the lever again and again with no results. He looked into the chamber of the rifle and found the magazine empty!

"Great Scott!" Roc told his friends later. "I was in for it. That durned bear come toward me with every hair on his back standin' forward. Fire shot from his eyes, foam came from his mouth, and I never heard such growls as he made when he jumped for me. I turned tail and ran for the pulp road which I was sure Burt would be comin' down.

"When I got to the road, I snuck a look over my shoulder and, believe it or not, that there bear was grabbin' at my heels and coattail. I was so skeered I even threw my coat and rifle away. I was runnin' for my very life, and over and over in my head went everythin' I had done and shouldn't of done—and that was plenty.

"I took another look back, and that bear was still at my heels, his wounded leg swingin' back and forth as he ran, his mouth blowin' bloody foam on my pants. Man, was I scared!

"I come runnin' around a bend in the road and saw Burt, so I swung my arms over my head and let out a few yips. Burt stood up in the wagon and whipped the horses. The old wagon came rumblin' toward us, makin' a sound like all get out on the cobbles and roots.

"The bear hadn't been skeered o' me, but he stopped when he saw

Burt and the team, and made off in the forest. I just fell to the ground and lay there, for I was almost dead from fright."

When Roc recovered, he and Burt lit out after the bear. They chased him through forests and streams, but finally the wounded animal ducked into a swamp and disappeared. The brothers brought home a load of stone, but afterward Roc was so sick with fright that he couldn't do a stroke of work at home for several days.

He handed out some free information to Burt. "Always take your wife's advice," said he. "Keep your gun well loaded and never tackle a wounded bear with an empty gun. When I was runnin' down that road with the bear nippin' at my heels, I could see angels."

Roc Conklin may or may not be seeing angels now, for he has been in hunters' heaven for years, but bears are scarcer than hens' teeth around Wilmurt, for the bears have handed down stories of Roc's prowess from generation to generation. And they, like the Wilmurt folks, know that, whenever the ground trembles, the ghost of Roc Conklin is chasing bounding bears through the forests along the West Canada Creek.

THE PESKY CROWS

Bill Platt told the best whoppers in Forestport, though he enjoyed lively competition from Ed Harrig, who claimed he shot a deer with the ramrod from his muzzle-loader, and from Charlie Elliott, who boasted that he had once got a flock of geese drunk on mash and had picked out all their feathers. Members of the Harness Shop Senate who gathered at Sam Utley's or the checkerboard experts at Mollie Morrell's store usually sat up and took notice when Bill wandered into the village from his place up on the White Lake road.

Bill was a medium-sized old fellow whose back had been bent by years of carrying supplies while guiding sports in the woods. His speech was slow and somewhat halting, for he usually invented tales as he went along and it took time for him to select the correct word.

Bill had been hunting with Ed Abbott up around Old Forge one fall and they had shot a deer of considerable size.

"How big shall we tell the boys it was?" asked Bill.

Ed rolled his chaw from cheek to cheek and said, "I tell you what, Bill. You make it as big as you want and so will it."

Bill spent some thought on the matter and by the time he got down to the Harness Shop Senate he had put a weight on the deer which seemed fantastic to him, but the members withheld comment, much to Bill's disgust. When he could stand the suspense no longer, he asked, "How big did Ed say it was?"

Sam Utley looked up and answered, "Why, Ed called it a hundred pounds more than you did."

"Why, that lyin' old scoundrel," cried Bill, who left in high dudgeon with the laughs of the Senate ringing in his ears.

He came back to Forestport a few days later, but stayed clear of Sam Utley's harness shop. Instead, he chose to impart his latest information at Mollie Morrell's. Checker players were better judges of veracity than those scoffers at the Senate.

"Some years back," he said, "me and John Harrig was huntin' deer up in the woods near Twitchell Lake." He stopped and closed his eyes. "Let's see, that was five years ago next fall." When he opened his eyes, they shone bright with reminiscence. "As I was saying, me and

John was hunting and somehow we got separated. Well, after missing John, I hunted along sort of keerful like, but getting nary a shot at nothing, so I sat down on a big rock to rest up before going back to camp.

"All of a sudden I heard the most all-fired racket over across the gully on the next mountain. I couldn't figger what it could be, but I kept my eyes peeled, and purty soon I noticed a large hemlock was black with crows and every one of 'em flying around and cawing like mad.

"Now that sort o' tickled my curiosity, so I made up my mind I'd get over there and find out what the ruckus was all about." Bill paused to let his words sink in.

"Go ahead, Bill," said one of the checker players. "Stretch it."

Bill registered indignation at this request, but he wriggled to the edge of his chair and placed his hands on his knees. "I crept down along the side of the gulley keerful-like," he said, "and then crawled up the side of that there mountain. Gosh all hemlock, you should have seen the crows. Thousands of 'em." He fixed the group with his eyes. Maybe tens o' thousands," he risked.

The players made no comment, so Bill asked, "And what d'you think was bothering them there crows?"

"Make up something, Bill," laughed Mollie Morrell.

"I ain't making up nothing," protested Bill. "And I'm here to tell you that the biggest bear I ever laid eyes on was sitting on his haunches at the foot o' the tree, cuffing away at those durned crows and letting out roars you could have heard a mile. What did I do, did you ask? 'Well,' says I to myself, 'Bill, here's business for you. You must have that there bear.' So I put two extry slugs in my muzzle-loader, aimed the old gun across a log and hit that there bear right between the eyes."

"What about the crows?"

"The crows? They flew away with a whoosh that sounded like Crandall's Falls in spring." Bill got up to go. "You know," he said in parting, "I believe that durned bear thought that the crows killed him."

* * * *

News note: "Atwell Martin says there are just 272 less black flies at North Lake, by actual count, than there were at this time last year." *Boonville Herald,* May 31, 1888. Maybe Bill Platt had something to do with that, too.

IKE'S BEAVER

Time hung heavy for the guides between seasons in an Adirondack camp, so they sat around telling stories or inventing amusements to while away the hours. When Uncle Ike Williams showed up with his pet beaver, they greeted the elderly guide like a lost brother, for Ike usually could figure out means of entertainment.

Uncle Ike, a veteran guide and an honest man, had a weakness for betting. When a guide came into camp with two live wild beavers, Ike suggested a race between them and his pet. The young guides covered Ike's money, for the old fellow's beaver, though mighty smart, had grown too fat to be a sprinter.

Ike wished he had not been so forward, but he seldom lacked ideas. He toddled over to the whiskey corner and poured himself a stiff drink, and a glorious plan began to formulate in his mind.

"If a little good old stuff works wonders with an old feller like me," he told himself, "I wonder what it would do for a healthy young beaver. Blamed if I don't think it could make him win that race. I know it's foolish to waste whiskey on a dumb animal, but this stuff belongs to the camp."

Next day, before the race, Ike announced that he wanted to give his pet a rubdown, so he carried it to the cabin. Once there he fed the beaver a shot of North Woods whiskey which would have stimulated a dead animal, and carried it to the starting line.

Ike liked high-sounding phrases. "Speed to the goal," he told the beaver. "You carry the throbbing hopes and money of your master. Don't disgrace the worthy man who owns you and has lavished his time and affection training you."

The pet beaver started out like a bolt out of the blue. It galloped madly down the course, leaving its opponents so far behind that the guides gasped with astonishment. For good measure, it danced around in the woods after the race to celebrate the easy victory. Uncle Ike also beamed as he collected the bets and suggested more contests.

Beaver races became the chief sport in camp. Other animals were caught and pitted against Ike's champion, to no avail. Even handicaps were tried, but Ike would handle this situation by feeding his beaver a little extra whiskey. It got to the point where he was giving his pet enough liquor to stagger a veteran toper.

Al Ferguson had lost considerable money on these races, and he was puzzled by the joyful prancing of Ike's beaver after each contest. One day, after another Ike victory, Ferguson picked up the old man's beaver and got a whiff of its breath.

When he had cooled off, Al said nothing to Ike, but he decided that he would not only redeem the beaver from a drunkard's grave but would also get back his money. He rummaged around and found a bottle of Gold Cure which some sport had brought along the spring before to help make him a tee-totaller, and had forgotten to use.

Al watched for his chance. One day, when Ike was not around, Al seized the beaver and began to feed it Gold Cure. The beaver did not take kindly to this act of mercy. In fact, it tried to bite Al, but the guide succeeded in getting a liberal dose into Ike's pet before the beaver broke away and scampered into the woods.

When Ike went to "water" his beaver for the next race, the animal turned up its nose at the whiskey. Ike smelled of the bottle and took a taste. Pretty good. Tasted again. Very good. Tried it on the beaver, who fought it off.

This show of ingratitude made Ike durned mad. "Turn temperance reformer on me on the day of the race, will ye?" he cried, as he forced nearly a half pint of whiskey down the beaver's throat.

The beaver looked pretty sick at the starting line, but it dashed off in its usual manner and was ahead for a few yards. All of a sudden, its pace grew slower and its legs wobbled. Halfway down the course, it rolled over with its feet in the air. Uncle Ike, heart-broken, toddled over and picked up his dead pet.

Ike received no sympathy from the other guides. "It was your own fault, Ike," said Al Ferguson. "If you hadn't taught him bad habits he would be alive today." He paused to let this advice sink in before adding, "And I'll have you take notice that he started this race, even if he didn't finish, so we'll collect our bets."

Ike paid.

THE BEAR HOAX

Back in 1893, Hinckley and Prospect got a bear scare, for reports came in that a big black bruin was lurking in the neighborhood ready to attack man, woman or child. The women, being more timid than their husbands, kept the children inside and peeped out of windows while their men sallied forth armed with shot guns, rifles, revolvers and horse pistols loaded with "bear charge."

This event so tickled the funny-bone of William P. Dodge, the BIJAH of the *Boonville Herald,* that he broke forth in print with a bear story which brought repercussions.

"The denizens of this village," he wrote, "were alarmed at an early hour Monday morning by the hurried arrival and excited manner of F. M. Smyth of Hinckley, who brought the startling news that Colonel Van Etten's son-in-law, Mr. Maxim, had been badly chawed up by a bear.

"The story was that Mr. Van Etten and his family were surprised to see a huge black bear lounge along into the barn yard and start off with one of the lambs that stood there in the flock. He made rapidly for the adjacent lots, with Van Etten and Maxim in hot pursuit, one armed with a Winchester and the other with a Savage rifle.

"In the brush they became separated, each going in an opposite direction around a sharp elevation that the bear was tearing straight over. As they came around the base of the hill, each took the other for the bear and blazed away. Van Etten was unhurt, but the bullet from his Savage rifle passed through Maxim's hat, and plowed a furrow over the top of his head, laying him out.

"The ball from there went through a birch tree twenty inches in diameter and through an Italian's cabin and on into the Pitman pasture across the creek, where it went through a flock of turkeys, killing three, and wound up by killing a cow that stood near a big rock.

"In the meantime the bear came clawing down the hill, just as Van Etten was bending over Maxim to discover how badly he was hurt, and knocking him over, sent his gun flying among the rocks and rolling Maxim over and twisting him around a couple of times, biting here and there, he loped off and disappeared.

"A party was soon organized and started to look up the bear. After a long chase, through what was formerly called 'Niggerville,' across the Elm Flats, and over the 'rag wheel' into Shongum, they gave up.

"At present writing, we are unable to state just how seriously injured Mr. Maxim is, and if we had got our information from some men we would have sized it up as a bear story, but knowing the honor and integrity and the high esteem in which Mr. Smyth is held in the community where he is prominent in business circles, we know it must be an authentic account of the affair."

Ben Van Etten, the butt of the story, was a farmer who lived across the bridge on the Herkimer County side of the creek. He jumped into his wagon drawn by cream-colored horses, and went after Dodge, with the result that BIJAH pulled in his horns.

"Although the Colonel has quite a reputation for bear hunting and finding bee trees," Dodge wrote, "it appears this circumstance referred to was a complete fake, in fact, a genuine fairy story, conceived in the fertile or distorted brain of a man calling himself Smyth, who also claimed that he and the Colonel were about to close a contract for the iron bridge at Hinckley, with the view of converting it into an Italian boarding school and shooting gallery. He related how near the Colonel came to being an angel in a voice which was so heavy that it made him bow-legged to carry it around. Believing what he said, we wrote the statement, and learned too late that he had been over to Rozelle Holliday's eating mince pie and limburger cheese, and drinking hard cider until he was not at all responsible for what he said. We take this opportunity to say that the Colonel did not see a bear. If he had seen one he would have killed it, and lastly there was no bear there."

"PANTHUR"

Guides in the Adirondack foothills a half century ago were so accustomed to communing with the silence of the forest that they seldom became talkative and it was on rare occasions that they took pen in hand and tried to relate what to them were thrilling experiences.

E. S. Robertson, who spent much of his life guiding parties through the wilderness, finished up his days in Barneveld. A relative gave to the author some years ago an article on "Panthurs" which Ed had submitted to *Field and Stream* with a request that the editor "excuse my spelling and mustakes as I never had the advantage of school." The magazine evidently rejected the article. Here it is in Ed's own words, one of the few written documents to come from the pen of a foothills guide:

"When I was a small boy I lived with my Uncle J E S Wilkinson in the Town of Wilmurt Herkimer Co N Y and he was Supervisor and at that time there was quite a number of Panthurs as they were then called in the Adarondacks and there was a bounty paid for them. They had to be brought to the Supervisor and he would either burn head or if they were to be mounted he would saw a piece out of the skull and punch the ears and pay the bounty. There was a guide by the name of Jack Sheppard lived at Old Forge then called Fulton Chain who was a good hunter and got quite a number and at one time came to my Uncles with 9 the largest measured nine feet and five inches from nose to tip of tail. I was not at home when he arrived and the hired man Adam Orr Called Cap thought he would have some fun with me so he took the largest one and took a sawhourse and some straw and set it up in the grainery right in front of the door and sent me out to feed the Horses when I opened the doore there it was the head was frozen with the mouth wide open and the light was not verry good and beleive me it was some time before I fed the Horses since then I have been nearly as close to live ones but I don't think I was nearly as scared. Later I worked for A D Barber at Jocks Lake now called Honedago before the Adirondack League Club was formed Mr. Barber leased of the Airs of the Anson Blake estate the 97 Thousand Ackers of land and built a Hotell at Jocks Lake and hired the Guides for so much a month and let them out to Parties goeing back in the woods to fish or hunt it was all woods then we were 9 miles from the nearest house we sometimes went back where there were only one or two Parties went in a year the fishing and hunting was good back there then. When the League was formed there was a man by the name of Arthur Jenkins who became a member he was Editor of the Syracuse Hearold he came up and wanted to get a big Buck and wanted it hul and not cut up so Mr. Barber sent Fred Kruzer and me with him in those days we used to run deer with dogs we had three dogs one day Fred would put out the dogs and the next I would we would put Mr. Jenkins on a runway and then we would take another. One day Fred was putting out the dogs I put Mr. Jenkins on a runway and I took a small canue and went up the creek to another stillwater. I had not got to the place I was goeing when I saw what I took for a deer in the brush on the bank of the creek. I kept looking and saw a deers hoarn about 10 feet from the shore I thought then it was queer that one should be there alive and one dead and I knew that the one I saw the hoarn of was dead I could not see the body but the shape the hoarn was in I new he was dead I ran the canue up to the shoar and stepped out and left my rifle in the canue I crawled through the Alders and then I saw what had happened the Panthur had eaten the deer and eaten all he could and then scratched the grass and leaves and covered up what was left all but the head and it was a fine head I did not uncover the carcus as I knew it was in bad shape but I wanted the head so I took out my knife as I thought the Panthur had gone I skined out the neck and head as we always do when we are goeing to mount it I was on my knees and was almost through when I heard a slight noise and turned my head and there was the Panthur not 10 feet from me he was streached out in a leap over the Alders and all the time I had been at work on the head he had not been over 10 feet from me behind the bushes watching me with back to him I have often thought it was lucky for me he had eaten all he could or there might of been a different storry and I would not been the one to tell it as the Panthur jumped so did I for my canue and caught my foot on something and would of fallen on the canue but jumped and dove over the canue in the water I came up and got my rifle and laid down the bank and kept verry still and watched and about three in the afternoon I heard a twig crack and in about 10 minits heard him run I knue there was no use waiting any longer I took the head and went down whair I had left Mr Jenkins and we went back and incovered the carcus the Panthur had jumped on the Bucks back and tore the hide in strings he had eaten most of the hind quarters but had not touched the head Mr. Jenkins sent the head out to be mounted and the last I knew of it it was in the Hearold Ofice we went up the next morning and the Panthur had been there and eaten all he could and covered up the rest but we could not find the Panthur. the third night after that after dark I took the waterpail and went to the spring for water and I had to feel my way with my feet it was so dark it was about 100 feet to the spring I was about half way when something jumped out of the path and went off in the woods I supposed it was a deer but in the morning the tracks was plain it was the Panthur and I was not over 6 or 8 feet from him when he jumped out of the path.

"In the winter I worked in the woods at Piseco and one of the men Theadore Remonda lived at Morehousville and went home Saturday nights and came back Sunday nights he went down our log road about a mile and put on snowshoes and went across to John Shiners tote road and his wife would meet him with a horse & cutter and bring him back Sunday night one Sunday night Mr Rumbley the Boss and I were the only ones up and we were in the camp by the stove when the door flew open and Remonda dropped on the floor he was as if he was dead we straitened him up and he was all out of breath when he could speak he said did you hear him and we wanted to know what he ment and when he got so he could talk he said when he came to our log road he took off his snowshoes and struck them togather to get off the snow he heard the Panthur scream up on Gerundagut mountain about a mile and a half away he said he started and walked fast tuardes the camp and when he was a little over half way there the Panthur screamed back where he took of his snowshoes and then he said he started runing and as he got in sight of the camp which was but a short ways from the door he said he could hear the Panthur jumping behind him the next morning we saw the tracks and the Panthur had come withing 45 feet of the door but had not steped in the road but on the outside of it about 8 or 10 feet from it he came to theroad where Theador had taken off his snowshoes and had followed on the side of the road to within 45 feet of the door and had gone back to where he came to the road and jumped accross to the snowshoe trail and followed about the same distance from it till he came to Shiners tote road and followed it up to

Shiners Camp and they had a large woodpile covered with snow and Will Hofmaster was blacksmith and he got up early to fix a pair of sleighs and as he cme out the door with a lantern in his hand the Panthur jumped off the woodpile and went up over the Mountain that was back of the camp and was not seen again."

WALT'S TWO-WAY HOUND

Over in Gravesville, Walt Santcliff owned a hound which, due to an accident and some quick thinking on Walt's part, became the only two-way hound ever to live in the Adirondack foothills.

One June day, while Walt was hayin' it, a scared fox suddenly dashed across the field closely pursued by Walt's hound, which ran nose-to-ground keeping on the scent. Walt put down his scythe to watch the chase.

The dog, intent on his quarry, ran nose-on into the blade of the scythe and was divided clean as a whistle from tip of nose to tip of tail.

Walt, who was an expert at grafting, picked up the two parts of the hound and slapped them together. In his haste, he somewhat altered the anatomy of the dog, for it now had two legs sticking up in the air and two legs on the ground.

Walt always claimed that the operation had improved the hound, for it could run on one pair of legs until tired and then flop over and use the other pair.

VII. FICTION

A foothills tale can sometimes grow so tall
That fiction weaves a web around a fact,
Supplies an anecdote with what it lacked,
And sheer imagination conquers all.
So Prospect village, near the waterfall,
Becomes the New Jerusalem, its early name.
The voice I heard could lay no claim to fame.
My champion never raced in Goshen Hall.

But from the sounds and sights of boyhood days,
When limekilns smoked and glowed along the creek,
And logging in Gang Mills was at its peak
And decent fun was found in simple ways,
I've let imagination take control.
Pure fiction is my one and only goal.

NO NIGHT FOR SINGING

Grandmother didn't want me to go with Hughie. All during supper she talked against it without giving me an inkling of why she was objecting. It wasn't until I grew up that I found out that all women can argue that way.

Grandfather was a quarryman. Being Welsh, he was a good quarryman, for he had inherited the art from generations of stonecutters. The Welsh cemeteries near here are filled with slabs from his quarry. To be sure, some of them lean with the years and others lie covered with adder's-tongue and myrtle. The chapels beside them have long since been torn down or abandoned, but stone endures.

Hughie was a quarryman too. He wasn't over long from the old country. Like many young Welshmen, he wandered into our section of the state, for limestone deposits are common along our brooks and creeks. Grandfather took Hughie on. That was how Hughie came to live with us.

He was about twenty-five at the time, though he appeared older. Maybe that was because he was short and blocky. Hughie's face was so homely that it must have hurt him. But when he smiled, he was the handsomest man in the world.

Hughie wasn't smiling that night at the supper table. He sat there bolt upright on the edge of his chair, waiting for grandfather to serve him. Even after grace had been said and grandmother was spreading butter on the bread before slicing it, the way the Welsh do, Hughie said nothing. All during the meal, my grandparents were disputing my right to go with Hughie. It was only when grandfather settled the argument by saying, "Janie, I did promise the boy he could go tend kiln with Hughie tonight," that a trace of a smile cracked the corners of Hughie's lips.

We started across the fields, Hughie and I. Dusk draws its curtain quickly in the north country. I had milked the cows earlier and had turned them into the pasture. A tinkle of a bell told me that they were feeding near the stone wall where the grass grew lush and green. A deeper sound was the roar of the waterfall where the creek drops twenty feet before cutting through the gorge near grandfather's quarry.

The only silence came from Hughie, who was swaying along the cowpath in front of me, walking with that rolling stride that his short legs imposed upon him.

Uncle Davey was tending the kiln fire. I could see him walking impatiently back and forth.

"What kept you?" he asked by way of greeting.

"An old argument it was about John coming."

Davey grinned broadly. He didn't have to smile to be handsome. "Did mother sniff the wind?" he asked.

Davey's question simply did not make sense. Grandmother had lifted her nose only once and that was when grandfather had made his decision.

Hughie said, "Ah, yes. Women do find out things."

"And she didn't want John to come tonight? Was that it?"

"He is safe," was Hughie's comment.

If Hughie had not said this with such assurance, I probably would have been less prepared for what happened later. The three words caused me to glue my eyes on Hughie, and what I saw frightened me.

It was all over in a moment and Hughie was smiling at Uncle Davey, but in that moment I had seen the face of a fighter, or at least of one who would fight if pushed into a corner.

Uncle Davey didn't smile, though. I had never known him to be so serious. The expression on Hughie's face was troubling him, too.

"I'll be back later and bring some of the boys with me," he told Hughie. "We'll have a little sing."

I saw nothing wrong with this suggestion, for it was a common thing for men to gather around the kiln fire to help the lonely tender through part of his long night vigil. Sometimes the girls came too, and brought corn and roasted it beneath the embers. What a time there would be, with jokes and storytelling and singing and a little sly lovemaking where the glow didn't quite reach.

Uncle Davey had said nothing about bringing the girls tonight, and his suggestion about having a sing had sounded a little forced. And when Hughie said, "It is no night for singing," I sensed that there was something really wrong.

Uncle Davey went over the stile and started across the fields. I listened for his piping whistle, but no sound came. Evidently he, like Hughie, was in no mood for music. When two Welshmen refuse to sing or to whistle, something is seriously out of the way.

I was hoping that Hughie might let me in on his secret, but he evidently had no intention of handing me even one straw. So I settled myself on a block of limestone facing the kiln opening and watched him replenish the fire.

A limekiln is a wondrous thing. And grandfather's was the best on the creek. Built of limestone blocks, it rose twenty feet against the cliff and was just as wide from cedars to cedars. Like a fortress it stood near the bank of the creek, much as the castles of feudal lords overhung German rivers.

I had watched Hughie and Uncle Davey fill the kiln with stone a few days before. Filling kilns is an art which is no more. The circular openings in which the stone was calcined were fifteen feet deep and ten feet in diameter. The first stones placed in the kiln formed an arch upon which the tons of broken pieces would rest. Any miscalculation in the laying of the foundations would result in a collapse of the whole structure.

Hughie understood the importance of the arch as a supporting force. He always chose a keystone capable of bearing the stress and strain of its supporting members.

The hemlock sticks were burning briskly in the square opening at the bottom of the kiln and the glow from the fire tinged the smoke with a pink that was prettier than Aunt Gwennie's new dress. Fortunately, the wind was blowing gently from the west, pulling the smoke toward the creek. Hughie must have been glad for this, for an east wind meant much coughing from the kiln tender.

If Hughie was glad, he didn't show it. He kept piling fresh wood on the fire, but there was a stubborn hunch to his shoulders and anger showed in every stride of his bandy legs. And I began to realize that there were two Hughies, one the care-free, smiling, singing Welshman who was my friend; the other a sudden, powerful stranger whom I did not know at all. Sitting on the block of limestone, I felt cold and alone. I walked across to where Hughie sat and dropped down on the bench beside him. My impulse was to ask him to sing, for he had the best Welsh tenor I have ever heard, but one look at him made me postpone my request.

He sat with his elbows on his knees and his chin cupped in his hands, looking at the fire.

A shift in the breeze sent a whiff of smoke swirling around us. I closed my eyes and coughed. When I opened them, Hughie had turned his face in my direction.

"Ah, you it is," he said.

"Did you think it was Yr Ellyllon?" I asked slyly, recalling the many times he had told me that Welsh goblins of that name haunt tenders of kiln fires.

My attempt at humor fell flat. Hughie didn't even crack a smile. Instead, he said, "John, mind you, be careful about women."

There it was, part of the answer to grandmother's objections. A woman was in the case somewhere. But what had that to do with me? I was only twelve and was not interested in women.

Hughie picked up the jackknife that lay at his side and began to whittle idly on a stick of wood.

"John," he said, "it is not women like your grandmother and your Aunt Gwennie I mean. Angels they are."

And I sensed right away that he meant two kinds of angels, gray-haired ones like grandmother and young ones with pink cheeks and brown curls like Aunt Gwennie. Like a flash it occurred to me that Aunt Gwennie hadn't appeared at the supper table.

So I asked, rather guilelessly, "Did Aunt Gwennie go out for supper?"

"No," said Hughie, "that she did not do. In her room she was."

"But she ain't sick?"

Hughie seemed to be pondering. "There be two kinds of sick, John," he replied. "One is sick in the body. The other is sick in the heart. She has that kind."

"But why?"

Hughie did not seem to wish to satisfy me this time. But at last the answer came: "A good woman she is, John. She wants her men to be good. She wants me to be good."

"But you are good, Hughie."

Hughie scooped up a handful of shavings and let them sift between his fingers. "Is it nothing you have heard today, John?" he asked.

If I hadn't spent the whole day fishing up the creek, I might have been better informed, but Aunt Gwennie had gone for the mail in my absence, so I hadn't had a chance to hear the village gossip.

"Is it something bad?" I asked.

"Bad enough it is."

"About you, is it, Hughie?"

"You and your old questions, boy. It is fenced me in, you have. And maybe better it is for me to tell you. You know that wife of Jules Chabot?"

I spit the bad taste out of my mouth. I knew what the men called her.

"I see you know her," Hughie went on. "Well, that woman is come here last week when I burn lime. She is come two nights. She is want me to make love with her. John, I do not want her. It is no man's wife I want. I tell that woman it is home with her man she should be. Now it is everyone she is telling that I try to make love with her."

"But that ain't fair," I blurted out. "She ain't got no right to say things like that about you."

Hughie almost smiled. "It is glad I am you believe me, John," he said. "So does Davey, but it is different with the women."

Yes, it was different with the women. I suddenly remembered that grandmother had not spoken to nor looked at Hughie at the supper table. And Aunt Gwennie, who liked Hughie so much that the villagers were getting ready to ring the wedding bells for them, had stayed in her room.

The road to the quarry was suddenly filled with noises. I could recognize voices, though I couldn't see anything outside the range of the fire's glow. I had heard such voices before, because I often had been at the quarry when the French Canadians from Gang Mills had come with loads of hemlock and spruce for the kiln fires. They had usually been loud, laughing voices, filled with boasting and song. Tonight they were swelling with anger.

"Jules it is," said Hughie, rising. "He is come to fight me."

"But why?" I asked. "That won't do no good."

"Fighting over women never does good," said Hughie.

I sat and watched him. Hughie was strong and muscular, to be sure, but what chance would he have against a man like Jules Chabot? The logger was at least thirty pounds heavier than Hughie. He had a reputation for rough-and-tumble fighting. Suddenly I was afraid, not for myself but for Hughie.

"Ain't you afraid?" I asked him.

"Yes, John, it is afraid I am."

I hadn't expected this answer. Hughie was my hero and I wanted him to fight like the knights I had been reading about. I was disappointed and ashamed.

The men were in the glow of the fire now. There was Jules, big and bold in his checkered shirt with his trousers tucked into high boots. I could pick out Mose Defrere and Chink La Farge and others. And right in the midst of them was that woman. Her bright red dress was tight to her body and she walked with a motion that made me think of the eel I had caught last week.

Jules wasted no time. He peeled off his shirt and gave his trousers a hitch. The hair on his chest was thick and black and his biceps became hills as he clenched his fists and squared his shoulders. He spat a cud of tobacco to the ground and wiped his thick lips with the back of his hand.

"Well, mister," he said to Hughie, "are you ready to take your licking?" Jules' eyes were close together.

Hughie was standing with his back braced against the kiln and his arms folded across his chest. "It is no use for two men to fight over a bad woman," was all he said.

That was enough for Jules. No bobcat ever moved more swiftly than did that logger. His hand was on Hughie's shoulder and his breath was in Hughie's face. "You call my wife a bad woman? You who try to make her bad?" he shouted, twisting Hughie's shirt in his long fingers.

Hughie's face went white as chalk and my supper came almost to my mouth, for I felt sure Hughie was afraid, that he would suffer any disgrace to avoid a fight with Jules.

"Let him be, or you'll be sorry." For the first time I noticed that Uncle Davey had come back. Behind him were Ivor Roberts and Bob Jones Painter and most of the Welshmen from the village. And I knew that was what Uncle Davey meant when he had mentioned bringing the boys for a sing.

Jules did not let Hughie be. I can see him now, standing in the glow of the fire, the devil's own expression on his swarthy face. With a twist of his fingers, Jules tore the shirt from Hughie's back.

Hughie was a modest man. He never took off his shirt when he worked, regardless of the heat of the sun or the kiln fire. I was seeing his chest for the first time and what I saw caused me to draw back. Hughie was not hairy like Jules. That was what made the knife scars stand out so white against his skin, one of them straight across his chest, the other long and broad from shoulder to belt, the two together forming a cross.

Jules drew back a step or two and stared at the scars. That is how he missed the expression that had come over Hughie's face. I saw it clearly in the glow from the fire. Hughie's eyes had narrowed to pin points. His lips were drawn back so far that his gums showed above his teeth. Anger had painted his face crimson.

Before Jules could gasp his astonishment, Hughie's fists were beating a tattoo on the logger's hairy stomach. Hughie hit so hard and so fast that all I could see was a blur.

Jules was helpless against this unexpected attack. Hughie's punches doubled him up like a jackknife. The logger's long arms flailed the air weakly over Hughie's shoulders and his face was the color of pea soup. He crashed to the floor of the quarry, right at the feet of that woman.

It was Uncle Davey and Ivor who pulled Hughie off his victim. Even then, they needed the help of Bob Jones Painter before they could pin Hughie's arms behind his back. And all the while they were struggling with him, Hughie was making cries like a panther that had been robbed of its prey.

It was some time before Jules was able to sit up. Never in my life have I seen a more surprised expression on a man's face. He sat there, gazing vacantly into space, all the while pressing both hands to those parts which hurt him most.

Uncle Davey had succeeded in quieting Hughie. He squatted on a block of stone near the kiln, his face cupped in his hands. He had drawn what was left of his shirt over his nakedness.

Mose Defrere and Chink La Farge lifted Jules to his feet. The logger sagged badly in the middle, much like a sack of grain. His groans were loud as they led him away.

And that woman? She had run kiting the moment Hughie got Jules down.

It was no night for singing, so everyone went back to the village to spread the news of the fight. That is, all except Uncle Davey. He kept winking slyly in my direction.

"Are you all cooled down now, Hughie?" he asked.

Hughie raised his eyes. "Yes," he said, "and it is ashamed I am. What is it Gwennie will think now?"

"Why don't you go to her and find out?" asked Uncle Davey. "She has been standing near the stile over a half hour, waiting for you."

Hughie stood up as if Uncle Davey had put a firecracker under him. "Gwennie?" he asked. "She saw me do it?"

"I told her the whole story when I got home," Uncle Davey explained, "and she simply had to come and see that nothing happened to dear Hughie. But she wouldn't like you in that outfit. Here, let's change shirts."

While Uncle Davey changed shirts with Hughie, I strained my eyes toward the stile. And, sure enough, I could see a shape there.

"John and I will tend the kiln," said Uncle Davey. "You go chase Gwennie before she gets away from you."

Hughie's lips spread in the best smile I ever saw him make. He started toward the stile.

Uncle Davey and I replenished the fire. I poured out my troubles through the clouds of smoke that curled toward the stars.

"Davey," I asked, "why was Hughie afraid to fight Jules?"

"Was he afraid?" countered Uncle Davey. "I thought he did pretty well."

There was no use opposing this argument. I hated to think what might have happened to the logger if Uncle Davey and Ivor hadn't pulled Hughie away.

"But Hughie told me before Jules came that he was afraid."

"Did Hughie say he was afraid of Jules?"

"No. He just said he was afraid."

Uncle Davey stirred the fire with a long pole. "You saw the scars on Hughie's chest tonight?" he asked.

"Yes, indeed."

"Hughie told me how he got them. It was when he was boxing champion of Wales."

Hughie the boxing champion! I might have known, after what I had seen him do to Jules.

"A robber attacked him on a lonely highway," Uncle Davey went on. "Hughie had only his fists to fight with and the robber had a knife. You saw what the robber did to Hughie. What Hughie did to the robber has haunted him ever since. That is one reason he left Wales, John."

"Hughie—killed him?" I gasped.

"No, the man lived, but Hughie has been afraid of his own strength ever since. That is why he didn't want to fight tonight, John. He was not afraid of Jules. He was afraid of himself."

THE CHALLENGE SOLO

The summer I was thirteen, a gang of Italians came to New Jerusalem to build a spur railroad into grandfather's quarry. Their tar-papered shacks were eye-sores by day; but, after darkness had fallen, they glowed with the sound of the accordion, the guitar and folk songs of a sunnier land.

I squandered my days at the quarry, watching the pick-and-shovel gang. Grandmother forbade me to go after dark. Since the Italians spoke little English and no Welsh, she tucked them into a pocket of her mind labelled "furriners," a coverall word for people she did not understand. No coaxing on my part caused her to relent.

So, almost every evening, as dusk settled over the pasture which separated grandfather's barn from the quarry, I would stretch out atop the corncrib and listen to the guitars and the accordions and the full-throated singing. That is why I was the first person in New Jerusalem to hear Alfredo.

The music started late that Saturday, for the Italians had been visiting Tom the Bartend in the village. The night was warm and the wine intoxicating. The men sat in the glow from the doorways, smoking, chatting and singing. I sat up, for it was time for my weekly ordeal in the washtub.

I had hardly finished stretching when a new voice rose from the quarry. *Di quella pira,* it pealed forth like a golden trumpet. I knew the man was singing "Tremble, Ye Tyrants" from *Il Trovatore,* for Aunt Gwennie had spent two dollars for Caruso's record of this aria. Caruso didn't sound like this. His high notes were pinched up in the horn, while the voice from the quarry rang fresh and free.

"Beautiful it is," sighed a voice beside the corncrib.

It was Hughie, grandfather's lime-burner, who had spoken. Hughie was a singer in his own right. He also had heard Caruso from the family circle at the Metropolitan Opera House in New York. His opinion could not be taken lightly.

The trumpet-like tones had carried to the village. New Jerusalem folks were arriving by two and threes. Soon our barnyard was filled with a silent, listening crowd.

We were rewarded with solos from the tenor repertory—*Aida, Rigoletto* and *Tosca* and several none of us had heard. Long after the last note had died away and the lights in the shacks were dying one by one, the Welsh of New Jerusalem tarried to discuss the voice from the quarry.

Only one man seemed unimpressed. He was Dewi Davies, local lawyer and perennial winner of the challenge solo at the *Eisteddvod*. When asked his opinion, Dewi turned down the corners of his mouth.

"It is much loud noise in foreign gibberish," he scoffed.

I walked back to the house with Hughie. It was easy to match strides with him, for his legs were short and bandy. We were at the kitchen door when he asked me if I thought an Italian could be taught to sing a song in English. And I knew right away what he was thinking, for the *Eisteddvod* would be held at Goshen Hall at the end of the month.

Aunt Gwennie came to the door to tell me the hot water was ready.

"You heard what that Dewi did say this night?" Hughie asked her.

"It was sour grapes," said Aunt Gwennie.

"Somebody must beat this Dewi quick or we can't live with him."

"I am sorry to hear you are not going to try again, Hughie."

"The devil!" exclaimed Hughie in Welsh. "It is not that I will not try, but that adjudicator from Utica likes a big voice. That I do not have. And Dewi said the other day he would sing *The Lost Chord*. That is too big for me. I could sing something else, but people do want somebody to beat Dewi at his own solo. You heard the man who can do it this night."

"Never have I heard anything like it," Aunt Gwennie admitted. "Which one was it?"

I was much surprised when Hughie answered, "I think it was Alfredo, the silent one."

"But he has been here all summer," I reminded him. "Why didn't he sing before?"

Hughie shrugged. "Strange it is. Maybe Tom the Bartend's wine did it."

"And you wish to get this Alfredo drunk to beat Dewi at the *Eisteddvod?*" Aunt Gwennie's question had an edge.

"Drunk with song," said Hughie, not upset in the least. "It is for some reason Alfredo hasn't sung until tonight. Maybe he won't sing again, but I can ask him. I thought you could play the piano for him, Gwennie, and teach him 'The Lost Chord.' "

Aunt Gwennie turned on me. "John, get you into that tub before the water gets cold."

I obeyed, for I knew she was going to help Hughie.

I haunted the quarry on Monday, for I wanted to see how Hughie made out with Alfredo. They met at the waterbucket about ten o'clock and I was overcome with thirst at the same time.

Hughie ladled out a dipperful and offered it to Alfredo, who bowed and indicated that Hughie drink first. The Italian towered over us, a barrel-chested fellow with the arms and legs of a blacksmith. He took off his hat and mopped his forehead with a bandanna. His hair was thick and black, like his bushy eyebrows and the mustachios which tapered to points close to his ears.

Hughie drank and handed him the dipper. He downed a pint at one draught, picked up his shovel and went back to work.

Hughie was the sly one. He bided his time until mid-afternoon. Alfredo was leaning on his shovel. Sweat poured from his face and darkened his shirt. Unhappiness was written all over his countenance.

"Alfredo sings better than he shovels," Hughie said to Pietro, a gray-haired Italian who had spent ten years in America and acted as interpreter. "Everybody beard Alfredo Saturday night. Tell him it was wonderful things they said about his voice."

Pietro relayed the praise to Alfredo, who acted pleased.

Thus encouraged, Hughie launched into an explanation of the Welsh festival of speaking and singing which would be climaxed by the challenge solo competition.

Alfredo's eyes sparkled as he listened to the translation. He asked Pietro a question.

"He ask can he go to it," explained Pietro. "I tell him I think so."

"Tell him the people want him to sing one song in English for the ten dollar prize."

Pietro relayed the offer.

A frown crossed Alfredo's face. "No singa Englesa," he said.

"Tell him we will teach him English."

"No singa," said Alfredo.

I could hold in no longer. "Let him sing in Italian," I suggested.

"Hush, you," said Hughie.

As I said, he was the sly one. "Pietro," he said, "tell Alfredo there is one man who does not like his singing. That is Dewi Davies, the champion. He says it is loud noise in foreign gibberish."

"Gib—" asked Pietro.

Hughie made a bold move. "Like a monkey, Pietro. Dewi says Alfredo sounds like a chattering monkey."

Pietro should have been on the stage. His imitation of a monkey was perfect. I would have split my sides with laughter if I hadn't kept an eye on Alfredo. Pietro was watching him, too. That was why he was able to dodge Alfredo's shovel, which buried itself in the side of the ditch.

Alfredo was no longer the silent one. The bold mustachios bobbed up and down above a torrent of Italian. Veins stuck out in his neck and on his forehead. He beat his chest and waved his fists. He kicked the dirt, even spat at it.

"Alfredo mad like hell," Pietro told us. "He tear that man's heart out. He kick him. He spit on him. He show him who can sing best."

Hughie looked like the cat who had swallowed the goldfish. "Bring him to our house tonight at seven," he told Pietro.

It was Aunt Gwennie who answered the timid knock. Alfredo stood on the porch, hat in hand. He had scrubbed his cheeks until they shone, and his mustachios had been freshly waxed. At his side was Pietro, uncomfortable in his Sunday suit.

Gwennie ushered them into the parlor and sat down at the square Chickering. Alfred hovered over her as her fingers ran through "The Lost Chord." He read music well, so he was quick to catch the melody.

The words were another matter. Aunt Gwennie had devised a system of phonetic spelling to suit the English to Alfredo's Italian. Four lines were learned that evening. It was beginner's luck that did not carry through ensuing sessions. And Alfredo was hardly a model pupil. Through Pietro, he would protest that English was a vile, unsingable language. The song made no sense. It did not show off his voice, for only at the close did it have high notes to which he could cling.

If Hughie hadn't been such a stubborn Welshman, he would have let Alfredo sing some operatic aria, for a contestant in the challenge solo could choose any song he wished and in any language. But Hughie had set his mind on having Dewi beaten at his own solo and neither hell nor high water could budge him.

Aunt Gwennie was smarter. She didn't try to drive Alfredo too far. Whenever his temper got frayed, she put a red book on the rack and let him sing arias from the operas that he loved.

It wasn't until the night before the *Eisteddvod* that Alfredo mastered the words. Even then, his pronunciation tickled my funny-bone so much that grandfather had to send me to bed early to avoid Hughie's wrath.

I don't believe anyone in New Jerusalem missed the *Eisteddvod* at Goshen Hall. The St. David's Society had borrowed every extra chair in the village. Children were squatting in the aisles. Men stood against the walls. The windows were thrown open so folks outside could hear.

I listened half-heartedly to the recitations and solos from the stage. Applause was polite. Most of the people were waiting for the challenge solo competition. The hall was tense when the chairman rose to announce it.

Hughie was the first to sing. Manly he was in his new blue serge and brightly polished boots. His tenor was manly, too, as it caressed the opening notes of "The Lost Chord." It flowed like a smooth river until it came to the big climax, when it was not equal to the task. Hughie's high notes were forced and strained. Red-faced from his effort, he sat down to a thunder of applause, for grandfather's lime-burner was much liked in New Jerusalem.

The chairman rose again. "It is now my pleasure to present Dewi Davies," he announced. "Mr. Davies has been the winner for the past five years."

Dewi was tall, lean and angular. He nodded slightly at the spattering of applause.

I sat up straight when the accompanist pounded out the pompous introduction to his song. It was *not* "The Lost Chord."

"Dewi Judas," I spat out, not caring who heard me.

No one did, for Dewi's rolling bass was thundering out the great air from Handel's "Messiah," the difficult piece which had won him the championship the year before. "The trumpet shall sound," sang Dewi, and the hall shook with the tones that poured from his throat.

I looked up to see Aunt Gwennie beckoning frantically. I crawled over ten or twelve boys to reach her side.

"Hurry, you," she whispered. "Run home and get the red book on my piano."

Dewi was halfway through his solo before I could fight my way to the door. Luckily, grandfather's house was across the street from Goshen Hall. I was back with the book while Dewi was acknowledging the applause.

He stood there, bowing stiffly, his thin face cracked in a one-sided smirk that showed how smart he felt about double-crossing Hughie. A few boos let him know some folks didn't like it.

Alfredo followed Aunt Gwennie to the stage. She put the red book on the piano-rack and sat down on the stool. He stood, hands at his sides, glaring at Dewi, who had taken a seat in the audience. I felt the cold sweat creep over me, for Alfredo did not have the little book of words to guide him through "The Lost Chord."

I took a good look at Alfredo. He wore a swallow-tailed coat and pin-striped trousers. His bow tie and vest were white as snow. The bold mustachios were the only reminder of the laborer at the quarry.

He nodded to Gwennie. The thundering introduction told me why I had been sent for the red book.

"*Di quella pira!*" sang Alfredo, and all tyrants must have trembled before the sound. Confidence oozed from every pore of Alfredo's body. His hands alternately pressed his heart and gestured toward the audience. It was just as if he were playing a part in an opera. And, above all, rose the glorious tenor voice which filled the hall and poured out through the windows. He flung out the high C's and clung to them tenaciously, while the rafters rang with sound. The applause kept them ringing for five minutes, while Alfredo stood, bowing from the waist, showing his teeth in a smile of pleasure.

The adjudicator said kind things about all three contestants, but he reserved his chief praise for Alfredo.

"I have listened to challenge solos many times," he said, "both in Wales and in America, but never before have I been privileged to hear such a God-given voice as the one we have enjoyed this evening. This man is more than a mere singer; he is a great artist. It is with humbleness that I award him the prize."

Dewi did not wait to see Alfredo receive his award. I caught a glimpse of his face as he pushed his way to the door. It was contorted with rage and disappointment.

The audience made no move to leave the hall. Instead, the people shouted for Alfredo to sing again. New Jerusalem was treated to an hour of song that was never forgotten. Alfredo had to sing every operatic aria in the red book before the people would let him go. And, at the close, a hat was passed. It was filled to the brim with bills and coins and presented to Alfredo as a token of appreciation.

Alfredo wasn't at work the next morning. I was at Hughie's elbow when he cornered Pietro.

"Where's Alfredo?" he asked anxiously.

"He go away."

"When?"

"Last night. He hurry right back after he sing. He pack his things and take midnight train."

"Where to?" asked Hughie wildly. "We must go after him."

Pietro shrugged and spread his hands helplessly. "Alfredo never come back," he told us. "He was opera singer in old country. Something go wrong. He come here. He not happy. He save and save to go home. He not even sing, he is so sad. Last night Alfredo happy. He get money he need. He say he like America now, but he love Italy. He go back home. He never come back."

Alfredo dropped out of my world that day. I never heard who he was or what became of him, but I shall never forget how he sounded that night I heard him for the first time from atop grandfather's corncrib.

WRONG SCENT

Winter came early to New Jerusalem that year. Snow covered the ground by mid-November and the village tinkled with sleighbells, for it was a poor family indeed that didn't own a horse and cutter.

After Thanksgiving dinner, grandmother said to me, "John, it's a mild day. I think Carnation would like an airing. Stake her out in the driveway for a little while."

Uncle Davey didn't take kindly to this suggestion. To him, cows were evils which stretched a six day week into seven. Furthermore, grandmother's cow was sociable by nature. She broke out of her stall and roamed the barn at will, scraping her horns against his yellow cutter and leaving droppings where the horse-fancier was sure to contact them with his Sunday boots.

"I'm going driving this afternoon, Mother," he protested. "I don't want that cow in the way of my horses. The bays don't like your pet as well as you do."

"Very well," grandmother sighed. "John, wait until His Royal Highness leaves for the Basin before you take poor little Carnation out of her stall."

And I sensed from the tone of grandmother's voice that she didn't approve of Davey's driving companion.

Davey had been sweet on Jennie Williams Basin since midsummer. I often ran across them near the stile that climbed the stone wall to grandfather's quarry. Accidentally, mind you, for I would never spy on my uncle. And sometimes, when dusk was stealing down to shorten the day, he would wander down the road that led to the Basin, a great hollow near the waterfall. At first, he took his fishpole and creel along. One evening I tagged after him, but he sent me home early, saying he wanted to fish a while longer. When I stopped to rest halfway up the hill, he was leaning on the gate talking with Jennie and I feared the fish weren't biting as well as he thought they would. The fishing habit became so strong that he wandered into the Basin after the trout season was over. He never asked me to go with him.

And on Sundays and holidays he would hitch up the bays and drive into the Basin. Sometimes I'd take a walk down there to pick raspberries or apples or to see how the gristmill looked when the wheels weren't running. I never saw Davey's rig in front of Jennie's house, but she never seemed to be at home, either.

Jennie was a little thing with lips like raspberries and a nose that turned up just enough to make it saucy. A ripe peach might have been jealous of her cheeks. That she wore her clothes well, even a boy of thirteen could see. Yes, Jennie was a picture from the top of her hat to the boots that peeped daintily from the hem of her skirt. Seeing her in Welsh chapel, I sometimes wished I were older and I would feel sorry for myself.

But not for long, mind you, for I had been combed once or twice by this same Miss Jennie. How did I know that my dog was going to bury his choicest bone in her tulip bed? Or was I to blame if I dodged Bob the Dingle's snowball just in time to have it send her best hat into a puddle of slush? What I did learn was that Jennie Williams Basin had a tongue that was tied loosely and could wag faster than the pendulum on our kitchen clock. If I had not been expert at dodging, my cheek might have been reddened by the back of her hand.

Two days before Thanksgiving, Davey, in a moment of confidence, had shown me a ring he had brought back from Utica. It was a thing of beauty, with a rock in the center that must have used up the earnings of a whole summer. When I asked him if he thought Jennie would like it, he winked an eye and said, "John even the best hound can sometimes follow the wrong scent."

I wondered if Davey had the sparkler with him, but he stormed out of the house so fast that I couldn't notice whether his pocket bulged or not.

I waited until Davey hitched up his bays and left for the Basin. Carnation seemed docile enough as I led her from the barn. She headed for a few wisps of grass that had been uncovered by the blades of the cutter. If I hadn't had business in the house I might have obeyed grandmother. As it was, I neglected to tie Carnation.

My inspection of Davey's room confirmed my suspicions. In his haste, my uncle had forgotten the ring. There it lay in its box, right on top of his dresser. I put it on my little finger and walked over to the light to see the diamond sparkle. If I hadn't been at the window, Davey would have caught me for sure and I would have been humiliated beyond words, for I wouldn't have pried into his affairs for anything in the world. Not intentionally, mind you. That was why I was glad to be able to see him drive up with Jennie. I was sitting in the kitchen when he took the stairs three at a time. There was a bulge in his coat pocket when he came down.

I pushed aside the curtains to see what was going on outside. What I saw made my heart jump into my throat!

Jennie was sitting bolt upright in the cutter, her hands tight about the reins, her lips set in a straight line. Davey's bays were prancing up and down like the horses I had seen in the circus in Utica. Out in front of them romped Carnation, kicking up her heels and making sounds that would have frightened any horse in Oneida County.

"Whoa!" yelled Uncle Davey, whose feet scarcely hit the snow as he ran for the road.

The sound of his voice was the impetus the bays needed. They bolted as one horse and pulled Jennie toward the dashboard, where she hung on for dear life.

Maybe Carnation had been fooling. I'm certain she hadn't been far-sighted, for she had no sooner finished kicking up her heels when the off bay hit her amidships. Grandmother's cow did a complete somersault and landed on her tail in a snowdrift.

Up the street the horses galloped, with Jennie holding tightly to the reins. They outdistanced Davey, whose boots slipped and slid on the hard-packed snow.

"Oh, oh," cried grandmother, wringing her hands. "Poor Carnation has been hurt and the Lord only knows what will become of that Jennie." She turned her wrath on me. "John, you careless boy, why didn't you stake Carnation out the way I told you to?"

It was no time to answer her question. I legged it up the street after Davey.

One runner of the cutter screeched when the horses took a turn about the triangular village green. The other was a foot in the air. My heart skipped a beat as the cutter righted itself with a jar which must have rattled Jennie's teeth.

She was doing nobly. Her initial fright had given way to anger. Her face grew redder than the pompon on her hat and the lips that were usually so full were a thin line. Though she was tiring, she might have gotten the bays under control on the rise, for they hadn't been worked much and were getting winded. I knocked Bob the Dingle down later and rubbed his face in the snow, but that was too late to prevent him from throwing the snowball. The white missile sailed over the head of Jennie Williams Basin and struck the off horse smartly on the rump.

The bays took the hill as if it were level ground. Davey made two futile efforts to grasp the bridle of the off horse. The second try sent him sprawling.

Men rushed from the stores and taverns. Their shouting spurred the bays to greater efforts. They took the corner of the green at race-track speed. They did, but Jennie didn't. Most of the males of New Jerusalem discovered that her petticoats had ruffles on them, for she landed head-first in a soft drift.

Davey helped her out of the snow, though I'll admit he used more courage than I would have shown under similar circumstances.

Jennie didn't wait to wipe the snow from her face or to straighten the pompon on her hat. It drooped over her forehead as she talked.

And how that girl did talk!

"Davey Meredith," said she, "of all the bungling idiots I've ever known you are the worst and I don't think there'll ever be another such nincompoop born in this village or any other one and if there is I hope someone has sense enough to put him out of his misery before he grows old enough to ask me to go riding and then turns a cow loose on the horses and makes them run away and isn't man enough to stop his own horses and they turn the cutter over and toss me out into the snow and make me the laughing stock of the whole village. And let me tell you, Davey Meredith, that this is the last time I'll ever ride in your cutter or your buggy or your carryall or in anything you have ever owned or will ever own and if you as much as dare to try to speak to me again I'll slap you across the mouth even if it is in chapel on Sunday."

Uncle Davey stood there, spellbound. He opened his mouth twice, but closed it again, for he must have sensed that he couldn't squeeze a word in edgewise. He was opening it for a third try when Jennie swung into action. Davey was no good at dodging. The back of her hand was across his right cheek even before his other one had begun to redden where her palm had slapped it. According to Griff the Store, who was the local authority on boxing, it was the best one-two ever delivered in New Jerusalem.

Having spoken her mind, Jennie Williams Basin picked up her skirts and ran down the hill toward the Basin, caring not a fig whether her ruffles showed or not.

* * * * *

Grandmother sent me to bed without my supper. I couldn't catch a wink, for the consequences of my negligence were pointing fingers at me in the darkness.

I gave scarcely a thought to Carnation, for grandmother's cow had escaped with a shaking up. She deserved that. Nor did I feel sorry for Jennie Williams. That girl had shown her real colors.

It was Uncle Davey who kept sleep from me. His cutter had no sooner been righted when he had stepped in and clicked to his bays. They had started toward Gang Mills at a brisk trot, trailing behind them the guffaws of the bystanders. That hamlet was the root of all evil, according to grandmother. In Gang Mills, loggers drank the bars dry every night. They fought in the streets, with knives and guns, as well as with fists. Davey was no fighter. He hadn't been able to dodge Jennie's one-two. He might come home torn to ribbons. He might never come back!

Davey was like a father and a brother, rolled into one. Grandmother was forever scolding him for spoiling an orphan. And when I got into trouble at school, which, sad to relate, was quite often, it was Davey who got things straightened out before news of my escapades reached grandmother's ears.

I sat bolt upright in bed. "I've got Davey into this mess," I said aloud. "I've got to get him out of it."

The clock in the livingroom below boomed twelve times. I slid my legs out of bed and pulled on my clothes. I tip-toed down the stairs, stopping once or twice to hold my breath when a board creaked.

The crunching of my boots on the snow told me that the night was crisp. As I hurried up the slope toward the center of the village, the darkness pressed around me like an icy blanket. In my haste, I had forgotten my reefer. I dared not go back after it.

Lights flared in the Union Hall. Men laughed and joked at the bar. Davey wasn't there. I must have been careless, for Tom the Bartend caught me at the window.

He opened the door. "John," he asked, "what are you doing out at this time of night? Go right home or I'll tell your grandfather."

I was afraid of Tom the Bartend, so I ran as fast as I could, but not toward home. Soon I was on the lonely road that led to Gang Mills, over two miles away. The wind whistled across the empty fields, carrying with it particles of snow which slapped against my cheeks and froze on my eyebrows, but I pressed my chin against my chest and plodded on. The wind rose. Swirls of snow caught me. I staggered when my feet encountered piles that had swept in from the fields. My shirt and pants were stiff with ice. Numbness crept into my hands. I walked as if I were on stilts.

I must have gone half-way to Gang Mills when the hopelessness of my mission struck me. If Davey had gotten into a fight with the loggers, what could I do about it? There was one thing I could do. I could get him into the cutter and drive him home. I wedged my tongue between my teeth to still their chattering. Turning my back to the wind, I struggled on through the night and the darkness.

If I hadn't been walking backward, I would have been run down for sure. As it was, I didn't hear the horses approaching. Their noses almost brushed my cheek when I shrieked and jumped aside. The next thing I knew I was sitting in Davey's cutter with the bearskin robe over me. He was turning the bays around in a driveway. We were almost in New Jerusalem before he spoke.

"Getting warm, John?" he asked.

I sat buried to my nose in the robe. The ice was thawing off my clothes, leaving me wet and clammy.

"I'm 'most roasted," I grumbled.

"Go ahead and roast." Davey's voice sounded grim.

He pulled up at the Union Hall, where Tom the Bartend stood in the doorway, his hands wrapped in his apron. The group of men behind him looked anxious.

"Where'd you find him?" asked Tom.

"Up near the Pitler place. Nearly ran him down. I'm getting him to bed before he catches his death of cold. Thanks for the help, Tom."

Davey clicked to the bays. We were in the barn in a few minutes.

"Sit tight," said Davey, "while I unharness the bays."

I was stewing in my own juice. "Do you want me to bed 'em down?" I asked.

"Don't you think you've helped me enough for one day?"

He took his own sweet time with the bays. He even stopped to look at Carnation.

"Is your grandmother's cow all right?" he asked.

"Uh-uh." I didn't dare say more for fear of touching him off.

"Get down and scoot for the house. Wait for me in the kitchen."

"Why?"

"Never mind. Do as I say."

I scooted.

The kitchen was warm and dark. I jumped when the clock struck twice.

Davey came in, lantern in hand. He closed and locked the door. "Take the lantern," he whispered. "I'll carry you upstairs."

"I'm no baby. I can walk."

"Yes, and wake up the whole house. Shut up and do as I tell you for once."

It didn't take long to change into my nightshirt. When I was between the feathers, Davey sat on the edge of my bed.

"John, what in tarnation were you up to?" he whispered.

I told everything, scolding myself with every other sentence. "And you're stuck with that ring, too," I blurted. "It was all my fault. If I'd tied Carnation the way grandmother told me——." I put my head under the comforter, I was that ashamed.

There was a moment of silence before the bed shook with Davey's suppressed mirth.

"The ring?" he chuckled. "Gad, John, that's wonderful!" He nearly choked as he strove to keep his laughter from waking grandmother. "And you thought I was up at Gang Mills drowning my sorrow because Jennie slapped me?"

My dander rose. I had been through the most gruelling experience of my life. If Davey hadn't come along when he did, I would have become lost in the swirling snow. This was the reward I got. Laughter! I'd have peeled him to the bone if he hadn't got in the first word.

"John," he asked, "why wasn't I coming from Gang Mills when I nearly ran you down?"

I let that one sink in. Davey had turned the bays around in the Pitler driveway. He had been coming from New Jerusalem. I had nothing to say.

Davey became serious. "John," he said, "I'm going to tell you about that ring. I got it in Utica. I showed it to you because I thought you'd like to see it. And you put two and two together and decided I was going to give it to Jennie, didn't you?"

My silence told him he was right.

"Lots of other folks got fooled the same way," he went on. "Jennie and I have had good times together, but a fellow should be able to take a girl riding without thinking of marrying her. Even in New Jerusalem."

"But," I protested, "the ring—"

"Jennie's brother Dick works in Gang Mills. He went to Utica last week and bought a diamond for his future wife. The jeweler had to set it for him. I picked up the ring for Dick on Tuesday. Jennie and I had planned to deliver it to him this afternoon. That's why I went to Gang Mills after the cutter tipped over. I came right back, John, perfectly sober."

"But you didn't come home for supper and—"

"Jane Pugh thought it would be nice if I helped eat some of their cold turkey for supper. She insisted that I stay for the evening. I was coming home when Tom the Bartend told me you had gone kiting off toward Gang Mills without your reefer. I want you to get everything straight, so you won't go sniffing on the wrong scent again."

I raised my head from beneath the covers. "Like some good hounds?" I asked sheepishly.

"Like some good hounds, John." He was still chuckling as I heard him get ready for bed.

THE MELANCHOLY WALKER

Jack Jones Quarry was walking champion of New Jerusalem. That was in the horse-and-buggy days, when walking was a necessity. Jack was Welsh and Quarry was not his surname. In those days New Jerusalem was a Welsh settlement. The Welsh wasted little time in seeking original names for their children.

As a result, there might be five or six men in the village with the same names. To distinguish one man from another, the Welsh tacked on either the man's trade, the name of his house, or the locality in which he lived. Hence, when Jack Jones Quarry was mentioned, everyone knew which Jack Jones was meant.

Jack wasn't an ordinary quarryman. He was an artist in stone. His little shop stood at the entrance to grandfather's quarry. Jack was a familiar sight on a summer day, standing in front of his shop with chisel and hammer, carving out the Welsh inscriptions on the limestone slabs that give a touch of immortality to those who have passed on. Jack had his own system for decorations—crossed guns and sabers for Civil War veterans, oak wreaths for orinary folks, lambs for little children. He carved them all with an air of reverence and often shed a tear over the little lambs.

Maybe that was because he had lost his two little boys in the creek. Jack became a drinking man from that day. It was a common sight to see him in his cups of an evening, or to hear him singing Welsh hymns at the top of his voice as he passed our house on his way home. The neighbors said Jack was a light sleeper. Even the barking of a dog would cause him to lie awake for hours.

That is how Jack Jones Quarry became the walking champion of New Jerusalem. After counting sheep vainly for an hour, he would set up, put on his clothes, and walk several miles through the countryside, "walking himself to sleep," according to his neighbors.

It was at Goshen Hall, the center of activities in New Jerusalem, that Jack heard about heel-and-toe walking. Two young fellows from Utica came up one night and gave an exhibition in the long, narrow hall that formed one wing of the inn. At first the natives howled with laughter at such antics. They were used to straightforward walking with no frills. These Utica fellows were using not only their legs but their arms and their heads. It was all too funny for words. Yet there was something contagious about it. Young farmers began to take the floor. They tried their best cross-country strides, but were soon outdistanced by the city slickers.

If there is anything a small villager hates, it is to have someone from the city outclass him in anything. Soon half the male population of New Jerusalem was out on the floor of Goshen Hall, imitating as best it could the peculiar antics of the two men from Utica.

The germ had been planted. From that night on, New Jerusalem became the heel-and-toe capital of Oneida County. Everyone walked heel and toe, from Grandpa Merriman down to the smallest boy in the village. It was a natural thing that Jack Jones Quarry, the veteran of many a nocturnal hike, should take to the new fad. It was also a foregone conclusion that he should win every contest held at Goshen Hall during the following months. The time had come to seek opposition from the surrounding countryside.

Matt Fanning was running Goshen Hall at the time. Matt was one of those men who could see beyond the ends of their noses. He sensed that the heel-and-toe craze would run its course. He wanted to capitalize on it while the griddle was hot. So he took the village by the horns one night by offering a fifty-dollar prize to the winner of an all-county heel-and-toe contest he intended to run off in his hall.

Flaming posters appeared as if by magic in New Jerusalem and the neighboring villages. Even Utica and Rome had a few, though no one expected city slickers to lower themselves by competing with country bumpkins. The posters proclaimed the time and length of the contest. One hundred miles, they said, in four nights, the first walker to complete the distance to be the winner of the fifty dollars.

Despite the ballyhoo, entries came in slowly. The reputation of Jack Jones Quarry had been carried for a radius of twenty miles, and few heel-and-toe specialists cared to match strides with the champion of New Jerusalem. Up to the day of the contest only Long Bill Hanks, the Boonville champion, had dared to enter the lists. This entry whetted the appetites of Jack's followers, for Hanks had beaten every heel-and-toe walker north as far as Watertown and had finished second to a touring expert from New York.

Jack trained faithfully for the contest. It was late in the fall, and the quarry was preparing to shut down for the winter, so our champion had plenty of time on his hands. I can see him now, bouncing along the road with his chin stuck out in front of him like the prow of a schooner, and his arms driving piston fashion ahead of his bandy legs. Crowds gathered in front of the general store to lend him encouragement and small boys imitated his style. Strangers from Boonville watched him carefully and accepted odds on their money.

Jack also gave up drinking, for the rumor had come through that Long Bill Hanks was a teetotaler with a remarkable record for endurance. Jack had always weakened on the last few laps, but he had usually been so far ahead of his competitors that tiring on the stretch had not hurt his chance of winning. He was taking no risks this time, for he would never be able to live down a defeat at the hands of the Boonville walker.

The day of the race dawned bright and sunny. Rigs of all description began to descend upon New Jerusalem right after noon. The afternoon train brought in heel-and-toe enthusiasts from Utica and all the intervening villages. Matt Fanning's wife had to serve the evening meal in three sittings. Matt engaged three men to satisfy the enormous thirst that congregated around his bar.

Long Bill Hanks appeared, flanked by two sports in loud checks. He was so tall he had to stoop in order to get through the door. There was an easy smile on his dark face and a confidence in his manner which brought the Utica money to his side. Matt arranged the bets.

The hall was filling rapidly. Rows of benches had been set the length of the room and the stage at one end was full of seated spectators who had paid ten cents a head to see the race. Grandmother had opposed my going. Taverns were no places for boys, said she. Uncle Davey had won her over by promising to keep tabs on me. So we wedged ourselves between Ivor the Hill and Bob Jones Painter and watched the people crowd into every possible inch of space.

Matt Fanning had been barker for a traveling circus in his younger days. He had not lost his flair for showmanship. "Ladies and gentlemen," he thundered, silencing the crowd, "we are gathered here to see the greatest exhibition of heel-and-toe walking ever to be put on in any community." Here Matt introduced several well-dressed strangers and led us in applause. "The race will be over a one-hundred-mile course and will be in four parts. The first quarter will be run off this evening and will be finished when the leading walker completes twenty-five miles. The other contestants will be given credit for whatever distances they cover and will start at that point tomorrow evening." There were more rules, but they were too complicated for me, so I kept my eyes peeled on the lane through which the contestants would walk to the stage to be introduced.

A gasp of astonishment went up from the crowd. Jack Jones Quarry was swaying down the lane with that peculiar rolling stride that was so familiar to all of us. Behind him came Long Bill Hanks, who towered head and shoulders over our champion.

The reason for the gasp followed. He was a little man, not much over five feet tall, dressed in hunting costume of doeskin with beads on his coat and fringe along the seams of his trousers. His moccasins made no sound on the boards.

The three contestants joined Matt on the stage. Matt introduced Jack first, for he was the local favorite. The roar of applause was so heavy that dust sprinkled down from the rafters. Long Bill got a polite reception, for he was a man both to be feared and to be respected.

Matt held up his hand. "There has been a third party at the last moment," he announced. "I'd like to introduce the reigning champion of St. Lawrence County, Mr. Romuald de la Fontaine, who is not only the heel-and-toe champion of that vast forest to the north of us, but also its leading trapper. It is surely a pleasure to know that our contest has attracted a man of such prominence. Let's give him a big hand."

We all liked Matt and hated to embarrass him, but the spattering of handclaps sounded like applause for a speaker at a meeting of the Ladies' Aid. Everyone knew the contest was to be between Jack and Long Bill. What right did a man from St. Lawrence County have to horn in at the last moment?

Mr. Romuald de la Fontaine took off his cap and bowed from the waist. Gold teeth flashed with his smile. "Merci," was all he said. Uncle Davey explained to me that meant thank you in French, for I thought the man was asking for sympathy.

Matt settled himself behind a table. Before him were three sheets of paper, for Matt was not only master of ceremonies; he was judge, timer and scorekeeper rolled into one.

The three men toed the mark. Matt gave the signal. Jack led off, using that bumpy stride of his. Long Bill was content to follow, though his steps were longer and easier. And what did Romuald de la Fontaine do? He waited courteously at the line, waved gracefully for his competitors to start, and followed at a polite distance.

He walked with short, dainty steps, much like a girl who is trying to show off her new Easter suit. The pace was slow, for the race was to be long and grueling: it wasn't the first few rounds of the hall that counted. The St. Lawrence County champion kept the pace easily, though he showed no desire to take the lead. Round and round the hall they went, ten times, twenty times, a hundred times. Now and then Long Bill would move ahead of Jack and set the pace, thus giving his supporters a chance to clap their hands and yell encouragement.

Romuald de la Fontaine seemed more interested in the audience than he did in the race. He smirked and bowed as he walked along. And I noticed that he was not a young man, for his hair was gray at the temples and long lines creased his leathery cheeks. It was almost impossible to see his eyes, for his perpetual smile pulled his cheeks up so high they seemed mere slits.

Well, they completed the first evening's trial in the same order they had started. A horse blanket would have covered them at the finish.

A heel-and-toe contest isn't too exciting to watch. By ten o'clock the bar was crowded with sweaty spectators. When Uncle Davey told me to go home, at least a hundred men were trying to buy drinks at the same time. Prominent among them was Romuald de la Fontaine, though I did not see him take a drink himself. Uncle Davey told me the next morning that the St. Lawrence County champion merely stood around listening to the men talk about the prowess of Jack Quarry and Long Bill Hanks.

Jack went straight home, for he did not trust himself at the bar. He was superb on the following evening, when he and Long Bill really let out. At the close of the second twenty-five miles they were far ahead of Romuald de la Fontaine, who had traveled along at the same mincing pace, despite the fact that he was lapped several times.

Maybe I got rather excited, for it was a wonderful sight to watch Jack and Bill struggling shoulder to shoulder all the way down the hall and back again. Anyway, I woke up some time during the night. Barking doesn't usually bother me, but this bark was the sharpest I had had ever heard. I crawled out of bed and went to the window.

It was a beautiful night, with the moon riding the sky and playing tag with the stars. I stood there, thinking what a night it would be to go out and cut corn or to help tend the kiln fire, but the corn was in the silo and the kiln wasn't burning on account of the walking race.

The wind was cool and I was about to jump back between the feathers when I heard a familiar sound. Sure enough, there was Jack Jones Quarry passing the house, his chin thrust ahead of him, his arms keeping pace with his legs. And I knew the barking had roused Jack from slumber and that he was taking a few turns around the village in order to get back to sleep. I didn't need that incentive. I hopped back into bed and dropped off.

The third night of the contest brought real fireworks. Jack started off like the champion that he was. His first spurt sent him nearly a half lap ahead of Long Bill, and he kept that lead half the evening, despite the fact that the Boonville flyer was putting everything he had into a supreme effort to overtake him. The crowd was on its feet, for here was an exhibition of heel-and-toe walking which was worth coming miles to see.

Only Romuald de la Fontaine seemed unconcerned. How he kept from being lapped continually was more than most folks could understand, but Uncle Davey, who had tried walking, whispered in my ear that the St. Lawrence County champion had lengthened his strides and was looking better every lap. No man who was ten laps behind looked good to me, so I paid little attention to him, except on those occasions when he stepped aside while Long Bill and Jack were passing him.

These gestures brought several laughs from the crowd. And it was funny to see that little old duffer look over his shoulder, grin, and then step aside and bow gracefully while his competitiors thundered on.

The bar was empty that night, for no one wanted to miss one second of the race. The walkers were approaching seventy-five miles now; three quarters of the contest were about over. Jack was leading by a few yards, but he was showing wear and tear. His breath was coming hard and his legs wobbled once or twice on the turns. Behind him came Long Bill, fresh as a daisy, his wide grin full of confidence.

Romuald de la Fontaine was about quarter of the way down the hall when the two leaders made their final bid. Down the course they thundered, arms and legs working overtime, faces streaming perspiration Romuald made the turn first and glanced over his shoulder. Halfway down the stretch he turned and bowed.

The gesture he made would have done justice to the court of Louis XIV. He extended one leg, swept the air with his arm and pressed it to his heart, all the while bowing his head before the oncoming rush.

Long Bill was on the outside, walking shoulder to shoulder with Jack. He was straining every muscle in an effort to finish the third quarter ahead. He tripped over Romuald's extended leg and sprawled along the floor. Jack, thrown off balance, managed to right himself and finish the lap.

Romuald was profuse in his apologies. He had only been performing an act of courtesy. If Mr. Hanks had sprained an ankle, he was profoundly sorry.

The supporters of the Boonville champion were not courteous. They were for lynching Romuald on the spot, but they were overruled by the New Jerusalem folks, who, I am sorry to say, were secretly glad that Jack's rival had suffered a mishap which might prevent him from finishing the race. Remember, they had placed odds on our champion, and money has a loud voice.

It rained hard that night and I didn't get to sleep right away, for I liked to hear the rain pounding on the roof. I hadn't snatched more than forty winks when that infernal barking started again. *Yip-yap, yip-yap* it went, something like a cocker or a fox terrier, but twice as loud. It sounded down the street where Jack Jones Quarry lived. I listened for a while and then the barking stopped. Being curious, I got up to see if Jack would go walking again.

Goshen Hall was right across the road from grandfather's house. I had no sooner reached the window than I saw someone in the road. The rain was coming down pretty hard, so I couldn't tell exactly who it was. I thought I had seen the man somewhere, but he ran into Goshen Hall before I could get my foggy brain wound up.

I was right about Jack. He came thundering up the street, going hell-bent for election, much as he had during that struggle with Long Bill which had resulted in the Boonville man's accident. The last I saw of him he was headed up the rise toward the general store.

Uncle Davey and I didn't miss the grand finale. We had to go right after supper, for the hall filled so fast that nearly a hundred people were left outside and the windows had to be opened so they could hear the excitement inside. While we were waiting for the race to start,

I heard Ivor the Hill tell Uncle Davey about Jack Jones Quarry.

It seems that Jack didn't come in until nearly sunrise. He was tired, wet, and thirsty. The bottle in the cellarway was very tempting. Jack went to bed and took the bottle with him. He would be in poor shape to walk twenty-five miles tonight.

Uncle Davey had put no money up on the race. He was too much afraid of grandfather to do that. Maybe that is why he didn't share Ivor's nervousness, for Ivor had staked two weeks' wages on Jack. And I didn't like the way Davey taunted Ivor by reminding him how much better Romuald de la Fontaine had walked the night before. I had seen Romuald make his curtsy. It had looked like a clean trip to me.

Matt made a special speech and the race started. Long Bill was there with his ankle bandaged tightly. There was a grimace of pain on his face as he left the mark five yards behind Jack. It was obvious that he could win only if Jack failed to finish.

Jack? He wasn't himself. That was easy for even a boy to see. His strides lacked rhythm and his face looked drawn and haggard. The pace that he set was so slow that Long Bill, sprained ankle and all, was able to match strides with him. We settled down to watch an endurance contest.

Romuald de la Fontaine had other ideas. The little man's gold teeth showed more often now as he lengthened his strides. It was a pretty sight to see him swing up and down the hall, cutting down the lead at every stride. True, he was fifteen laps behind, but it was he who was doing the passing now, and he had a new gesture of courtesy for that situation. No bows and extended leg now, mind you, only an exasperating grin and a salute in passing.

With five miles to go, Jack seemed to get his second wind, or else his head was clearing. Distance began to show between him and Long Bill, who was limping badly. The partisan crowd, sensing that Jack was to win, broke forth in wild applause.

Romuald de la Fontaine may have heard the cheers and handclapping, but he merely stuck to his knitting. And it was noticeable that he was walking about twice as fast as Jack, that he had cut our champion's lead to three laps. Long Bill had dropped out of the race with five laps to go. Romuald de la Fontaine had passed him two miles before, when Bill's bad ankle had slowed him to a snail's pace. Bill dropped to a bench and glared angrily at the St. Lawrence County champion.

Romuald de la Fontaine was walking beautifully. Gone were the mincing, lady-like steps. Every muscle of the little man's body seemed to be shaking hands as he cut down Jack's lead.

Our champion was puffing. His legs were all over the course. Uncle Davey had to hold out his hands to keep Jack from falling on us when he took the corner. If ever a man was crying for a bed and a night's sleep, it was Jack Jones Quarry.

The last lap began with Ronuald de la Fontaine at Jack's shoulder. Through sheer stubbornness, Jack matched strides with his opponent halfway down the hall. The cheers of the crowd had been silenced, partly because folks sensed that the outsider would win, but mostly because nobody could talk above a whisper.

They took the turn together. Romuald de la Fontaine saluted Jack as he passed the local champion. The crowd could have been under one of Jack's gravestones, it was that quiet.

That was why the barking sounded so loud in the hall. *Yip-yap, yip-yap* it came, right from the lips of Romuald de la Fontaine. And I knew it was the St. Lawrence County champion who had run into Goshen Hall the night before.

Jack reacted to the sound like a dog touched with turpentine. His foot took Romuald de la Fontaine in the south end of the spine and lifted the little man clean off the floor. The St. Lawrence champion landed on all fours right in front of Long Bill Hanks. The last I saw of Romuald de la Fontaine he was sailing over my head and out the open window.

No one ever challenged Jack Jones Quarry after that night and the heel-and-toe craze died a natural death.

Goshen Hall went up in a cloud of smoke over twenty years ago.

Memories are hard to erase. Even now, on an autumn night, when a dog barks through the wind and the rain, I rise and go to the window to see if Jack Jones Quarry is taking a turn around the village. I never see him, for he is resting in the Welsh cemetery with the crossed guns, the oak wreaths, and the little lambs.

Most of the folks have forgotten that Jack was the heel-and-toe champion of New Jerusalem, but his handiwork may live forever.

There is something immortal about stone.

www.ingramcontent.com/pod-product-compliance
Lightning Source LLC
Chambersburg PA
CBHW070926010526
44110CB00056B/2164